A VERGIL Workbook

LLWS

Latin Literature Workbook Series

A Series Edited by LeaAnn A. Osburn

A Horace Workbook (2005)

A Horace Workbook Teacher's Manual (2006)

An Ovid Workbook (2006)

A Catullus Workbook (2006)

A VERGIL Workbook

Katherine Bradley
& Barbara Weiden Boyd

Bolchazy-Carducci Publishers, Inc.
Mundelein, Illinois USA

Series Editor
LeaAnn A. Osburn

Volume Coeditors
LeaAnn A. Osburn
Donald E. Sprague

Typography, Page and Cover Design
Adam Phillip Velez

A Vergil Workbook

by Katherine Bradley & Barbara Weiden Boyd

© 2006 with corrections Bolchazy-Carducci Publishers, Inc.
All rights reserved.

Bolchazy-Carducci Publishers, Inc.
1570 Baskin Rd.
Mundelein, IL 60060 USA
www.bolchazy.com

Printed in the United States of America
2009
by United Graphics

ISBN 978-0-86516-614-1

CONTENTS

FOREWORD

All Latin teachers want their students to read ancient authors in the original. Yet to study the authentic Latin of an ancient Roman author is a complex task. It requires comprehension of the text and its grammatical underpinnings; an understanding of the world events and the culture in which the work of literature was produced; an ability to recognize the figures of speech the author uses and to grasp the impact they have on the text; sensitivity to the way sound effects, including meter if a passage is poetry, interact with the meaning of the text; and the ability to probe whatever thoughts and ideas the author may be expressing. To be successful in this multifaceted task, students need not only a comprehensive textbook but also exercises of different kinds in which to practice their newly developing literary and critical skills.

Students often need extensive drill and practice material—something not available in the traditional Latin author textbook—to help them master the grammar and syntax of the Latin text as well as the literary skills that the text demands of its readers. Teachers, too, no matter how many questions they ask in class to help their students analyze the syntax and the literary qualities of the text, often need and want more questions to be available. Realizing this need on the part of both students and teachers, Bolchazy-Carducci Publishers has begun to develop a series of workbooks to accompany Advanced Placement textbooks. There will be five workbooks in the series, one for each advanced placement author: Catullus, Cicero, Horace, Ovid, and Vergil. A team of authors—one, a university scholar with special expertise in the Latin literary text and the other, a high school Advanced Placement Latin teacher—will write each workbook.

Workbooks in this series will contain the Latin text for the material on the Advanced Placement Syllabus and exercises that drill grammar, syntax, and figures of speech. In addition, multiple-choice questions will be included and will focus on the student's comprehension of the passage and on items of literary analysis. The workbooks will also feature scansion practice, essays to write, and other questions that are appropriate to the author being studied. By reading and answering these types of questions, students will gain experience with the types of questions that are found on the Advanced Placement Examinations. Students at the college level will also benefit from the additional practice offered in the workbooks.

These workbooks contain neither textual notes nor vocabulary on the page with the text nor on the facing page. The absence of these traditional features of textbooks will allow students, after reading the Latin passage in the textbook, to practice in the workbook what they have learned and to assess how much they have mastered already and what needs more study. The workbooks will, however, contain a Latin to English Vocabulary at the back of the book.

We are confident that this series of workbooks has a unique role to play in fostering students' understanding of authentic Latin text and will be a significant addition to the Advanced Placement and college materials that already exist.

LeaAnn A. Osburn
Series Editor

PREFACE

This is the second in the series of workbooks on Advanced Placement (AP*) Latin authors to be published by Bolchazy-Carducci Publishers. As collaborators on this project, we have greatly enjoyed the privilege of working on an author and a poem so dear to our minds and hearts. Our long friendship has indeed been founded on a shared dedication to the study and reading of Latin literature, and Vergil's *Aeneid* holds a unique place for both of us as a source of personal and professional inspiration. This common bond was reinforced in summer 2002, when one of us directed and the other participated in a workshop on Vergil for AP* Latin teachers, offered through the Taft Education Center but held in Rome, the city that, like Vergil himself, witnessed Augustus' ascent to supreme power, and that, again like Vergil, continues to be shaped profoundly by that historical event. Since then, we have spent many hours discussing how best to help students attain the same love for Vergil that we enjoy, and have been guided accordingly in our design of this workbook. It is a privilege to share the results of our labors with readers new to Vergil.

This workbook is designed to provide Latin students with exercises to accompany and support their reading of the selections from the *Aeneid* that form the basis of the AP* Vergil syllabus. It is not, however, purely an AP* workbook: we hope that its audience will include both AP* Latin students and others who, in any classroom context whatsoever, have reason to find exercises in close reading to be of use. Likewise, this workbook can be used in tandem both with textbooks designed specifically with AP* students' needs in mind and with textbooks that encompass a wider readership, including those commonly used on the college level. The Latin text used throughout this workbook is based on R. A. B. Mynors' Oxford text (1969; reprinted with corrections 1972), but incorporates the same cosmetic alterations found in B. W. Boyd, *Vergil's Aeneid: Selections from Books 1, 2, 4, 6, 10, & 12* (Bolchazy-Carducci Publishers 2001; second edition 2004): the initial letters of words beginning a new sentence are printed in the upper case; and third-declension accusative plural nouns and adjectives ending in **-is** are here printed as ending in **-es.** The vocabulary list found at the end of this workbook is based on the General Wordlist originally included in the form of an "extensible sheet" in C. Pharr, *Vergil's Aeneid Books I-VI* (revised edition 1964; Bolchazy-Carducci Publishers 1998).

The selections from the *Aeneid* included in this book have been divided into thirty units, or chapters. These divisions are not meant to hold great interpretive significance, nor do they necessarily conform to the divisions found in most textbooks. Rather, our goal has been to provide a lesson of appropriate length and complexity to accompany weekly assignments when spread out over an academic year of approximately thirty weeks. While we hope that this structure will add to the workbook's usefulness in the average Latin classroom, we recognize that few Vergil classes are "average" and that every teacher is likely to have a slightly different pace and set of priorities, as well as a unique group of students to work with, in any given year. The allotment of time suggested for answering some of the questions, therefore, is meant simply as a rough guideline; teachers and students alike should modify these suggestions in accordance with their unique needs and pace. Indeed, we encourage all users of this book to adapt it freely to their own needs and classroom settings, and to see it as a source of inspiration for their own creative innovations rather than as a prescriptive taskmaster.

* AP is a registered trademark of the College Entrance Examination Board, which was not involved in the production of, and does not endorse, this product.

In each lesson, we provide most or all of the following types of questions:

I. Comprehension Questions
II. Multiple Choice Questions
III. Translation Questions
IV. Essay Questions
V. Scansion Exercises
VI. Short Answer Questions

Under the last of these headings can be found a variety of question-types, including:

VIa. Translation and Analysis Questions
VIb. Questions on Figures of Speech and Rhetorical Devices
VIc. Identification Questions Covering Names, Places, and Historical and Mythical Characters and Events
VId. Questions on Grammar and Syntax

Some of these question-types (II–IV in particular) are based closely on the types of questions found on the AP* Vergil Examination. All of these question-types provide practice and review of the skills required to succeed on the AP* Vergil examination, as well as in other classroom contexts with other tests of proficiency. Our combined experience of many years with the AP* Latin program nonetheless makes it clear to us that, while the AP* Vergil test provides a thorough and reliable means to assess a variety of skills and types of knowledge, it does not presume to ask every possible type of question or to assess every measurable aspect of Latin reading comprehension. We have therefore provided many questions in this workbook that we are confident will make students better readers of Vergil, and that are at least sometimes meant to provoke thought in ways not easy to quantify through standardized tests. For an authoritative explanation of the format of the AP* Latin Examinations, including the AP* Vergil Examination, teachers and students alike are urged to consult the publications of the College Entrance Examination Board, available through its website (apcentral.collegeboard.com). These publications also include examples of some of the examinations administered in recent years, and a variety of supplemental materials to support the Advanced Placement experience.

I. Comprehension Questions

These questions ask, in an order that follows the sequence of the passage under review, about a wide variety of topics discoverable from close reading of the text. Some incorporate analysis of grammar and/or syntax, or draw attention to Vergil's diction; others require translation, interpretation, and analysis; and others invite the reader to express his or her personal reaction to a given event or scene. Many of these questions could be used as the basis for a more lengthy essay question should a teacher wish to do so; but as they stand, most of these questions can be used for homework or in-class assignments, to be completed by students working either individually or in small groups.

* AP is a registered trademark of the College Entrance Examination Board, which was not involved in the production of, and does not endorse, this product.

II. Multiple Choice Questions

Some of these questions ask about the same features as do the multiple-choice questions on the Advanced Placement Examination: translation or interpretation, grammar, lexical details, allusions and references, meter, and figures of speech. Others, focusing primarily on comprehension and translation skills, require a higher degree of precision about grammar and syntax than is normally tested on the AP* Vergil Examination; and some are intended for quicker completion, especially in those cases when the student is required to choose the correct response from two rather than four options.

As currently constituted, the multiple-choice section of the Vergil Advanced Placement examination consists of four passages: three "unseen" passages (usually one prose and two poetry) and one "seen" passage chosen from the selections on the AP* Vergil syllabus. Exercises in this workbook do not provide practice with the material found on the "unseen" portion of the exam; nonetheless, because students generally find the multiple-choice section of the AP* exam to be challenging, we believe that they can profit from the extensive practice with multiple-choice questions provided here.

III. Translation Exercises

These exercises test the translation skills of students who have been reading the selections included here in a Latin course. Some of the passages tested here are of approximately the same length as those found on the AP* Examination; others are longer or shorter. Even when not explicitly directed to do so, students should aim to provide a translation that is as literal as possible. For this reason, they should not change active verbs to passive voice or vice versa, or alter verb tenses. In translating the historical present, students may use either the English present tense for Latin present or consistently convert to past tense in English. Students should stay as close as possible to the range of standard definitions of words and should not impose from the context a sense that the word does not have.

IV. Essay Questions

Most of the essay questions in this workbook call for the in-depth literary analysis of a passage or entire selection. They are best undertaken either alongside the preparation and translation of the passages to which they pertain, or after students have already discussed the passage or selection in class. Some essay questions also draw on students' familiarity with the content of a given book as a whole, i.e., including those sections not read in Latin; when such questions appear, students should be encouraged to demonstrate their broader interpretive and analytical skills. Finally, at least one review question is included at the close of the series of exercises for each of the books of the *Aeneid* from which selections are included, i.e., at the close of exercises covering Books I, II, IV, VI, X, and XII. These questions are intended to offer students practice with the general comprehension essays found on the AP* Vergil examination, and invite students to synthesize their knowledge of the parts of the *Aeneid* read in English together with the Latin selections on the syllabus.

* AP is a registered trademark of the College Entrance Examination Board, which was not involved in the production of, and does not endorse, this product.

Wherever possible and appropriate, strong essay answers should

- address the question exactly as it is asked, especially if more than one task is entailed;
- analyze, not merely describe, the passage or selection being tested;
- address the passage or selection as a whole;
- and support claims and arguments with evidence drawn from the Latin text. In other words, when answering essay questions covering a specific passage or selection of lines, students should copy the relevant Latin words or cite the appropriate line numbers AND translate or paraphrase closely enough so that their comprehension of the Latin text is evident.

V. Scansion Exercises

Once they have learned dactylic hexameter, students can practice scansion with any excerpt from Vergil, whether or not they have translated it. Following the format of the Advanced Placement Examination, we do not provide macrons/long marks in the Latin text. We also include in these exercises some lines of unusual metrical difficulty, so that teachers may have the opportunity if they wish it to draw attention to Vergil's expressive use of metrical effects.

VIa. Translation and Analysis Questions

This question-type appears only occasionally, and is a logical extension of the Translation Exercises (see above, III). Students are first asked to translate, and in doing so should follow the guidelines for translation offered above in III. They are then asked to demonstrate how this translation can be used to support the analysis and interpretation of the passage under consideration.

VIb. Questions on Figures of Speech and Rhetorical Devices

The terms "figure of speech" and "rhetorical device" are used in this workbook to refer to figurative uses of language in general, whether they involve non-standard senses of words (sometimes called tropes or figures of thought) or arrangements of words (sometimes called rhetorical figures or figures of speech). We use these terms in the broad sense in order to encompass not only all the literary devices for which students will be held responsible on the Advanced Placement Examination, but also devices which do not appear on the current list of figures of speech to be tested on the Advanced Placement Examination. Because we envision an audience for this workbook that includes not only students preparing for the AP* Vergil Examination but others who wish to appreciate the poetry of the *Aeneid* to the fullest, we encourage readers to learn as much as possible about the techniques of Latin poetry by acquainting themselves with literary devices besides those on the current AP* list.

* AP is a registered trademark of the College Entrance Examination Board, which was not involved in the production of, and does not endorse, this product.

VIc. Identification Questions Covering Names, Places, and Historical and Mythical Characters and Events

The narrative richness of the *Aeneid* is enhanced throughout the poem by Vergil's use of proper names and epithets to designate characters, places, and events known from classical myth and/or ancient history and geography. While the current AP* Vergil Examination does not include questions that test students' specific knowledge of these names and epithets, we believe it is important to reward those students who observe such details by emphasizing this central aspect of Vergil's poetic diction. These names and epithets are often essential, furthermore, both to success in the reading process and to an appreciation of Virgil's artistry. Teachers may use these exercises if they wish as an opportunity to introduce cultural materials into their classes to enrich the context in which the *Aeneid* is studied.

VId. Questions on Grammar and Syntax

Sound knowledge of Latin grammar and syntax is fundamental to strong comprehension and translation skills. Therefore, although grammar and syntax *per se* are tested only on the multiple-choice section of the AP* Examination, and there only to a limited degree, we have included here occasional exercises aimed at keeping students' philological abilities as keen as possible.

* * * * * * * *

We close with an acknowledgement of all those who helped us, either directly or indirectly, with this project. LeaAnn Osburn, the series editor, invited us to prepare this workbook and has offered advice and suggestions at various stages of the writing process. Donald Sprague has applied his careful reading and critical skills to great advantage in reviewing and standardizing features of the manuscript. AP* Vergil students at Groton School, furthermore, cheerfully and patiently completed preliminary versions of many of these exercises and scrutinized with keen eyes the final draft. We are greatly indebted to David Ross, who scrupulously read and commented on the entire manuscript; both he and Margaret Brucia proffered guidance, encouragement, and critical support when our spirits flagged. The faith, optimism, and enthusiasm of Matthew McCracken kept spirits up even in the darkest moments; and the Boyds, both Michael and Rachel, cheered us on as is their wont. And last but not least, we are indebted to all our students past and present, especially those with whom we have had the privilege of reading Vergil, for sharing their insights, enthusiasms, and new questions with us, their teachers. It remains a joy for us, as it ever has been, to discover something new on each rereading of the *Aeneid*.

KATHERINE BRADLEY
Groton School
Groton, Massachusetts

BARBARA WEIDEN BOYD
Bowdoin College
Brunswick, Maine

* AP is a registered trademark of the College Entrance Examination Board, which was not involved in the production of, and does not endorse, this product.

THE *AENEID* BOOK I SELECTIONS WITH EXERCISES

LESSON 1: BOOK I. 1–33

Arma virumque cano, Troiae qui primus ab oris
Italiam fato profugus Laviniaque venit
litora, multum ille et terris iactatus et alto
vi superum, saevae memorem Iunonis ob iram,
multa quoque et bello passus, dum conderet urbem
inferretque deos Latio; genus unde Latinum
Albanique patres atque altae moenia Romae.
Musa, mihi causas memora, quo numine laeso
quidve dolens regina deum tot volvere casus
insignem pietate virum, tot adire labores
impulerit. Tantaene animis caelestibus irae?
Urbs antiqua fuit (Tyrii tenuere coloni)
Karthago, Italiam contra Tiberinaque longe
ostia, dives opum studiisque asperrima belli,
quam Iuno fertur terris magis omnibus unam
posthabita coluisse Samo. Hic illius arma,
hic currus fuit; hoc regnum dea gentibus esse,
si qua fata sinant, iam tum tenditque fovetque.
Progeniem sed enim Troiano a sanguine duci
audierat Tyrias olim quae verteret arces;
hinc populum late regem belloque superbum
venturum excidio Libyae; sic volvere Parcas.
Id metuens veterisque memor Saturnia belli,
prima quod ad Troiam pro caris gesserat Argis—
necdum etiam causae irarum saevique dolores
exciderant animo; manet alta mente repostum
iudicium Paridis spretaeque iniuria formae
et genus invisum et rapti Ganymedis honores:
his accensa super iactatos aequore toto
Troas, reliquias Danaum atque immitis Achilli,
arcebat longe Latio, multosque per annos
errabant acti fatis maria omnia circum.
Tantae molis erat Romanam condere gentem.

Comprehension Questions

1. In the opening line, how does Vergil allude to Homer's *Iliad* and *Odyssey*?

____

____

2. What does the poet ask the Muse to explain?

____

____

3. From lines 1–11, copy out and translate a phrase that characterizes Aeneas.

____

4. In lines 25–29, what are the three reasons Vergil gives for Juno's anger toward the Trojans?

____

____

____

____

5. How would you characterize Juno as depicted in this passage? Make sure that you copy out and translate at least three words or phrases that demonstrate features of Juno's character. Provide line references in parentheses for your three Latin choices.

____

____

____

____

Multiple Choice Questions *Suggested Time: 18 minutes*

1. The word *qui* (line 1) refers to (i.e., the antecedent of *qui* is)

   a. *arma*
   b. *cano*
   c. *virum*
   d. *Troiae*

2. The case and number of *superum* (line 4) are

   a. accusative plural
   b. nominative singular
   c. accusative singular
   d. genitive plural

3. In line 5, *dum* is translated
   a. while
   b. until
   c. provided that
   d. then

4. In lines 8–11, Vergil follows the old epic tradition of asking for inspiration from
   a. a muse
   b. the queen
   c. a pious man
   d. a divine will

5. The form of the word *tenuere* (line 12) is
   a. present infinitive
   b. present indicative
   c. perfect infinitive
   d. perfect indicative

6. The word *posthabita* (line 16) modifies
   a. *Iuno* (line 15)
   b. *Samo* (line 16)
   c. *ostia* (line 14)
   d. *arma* (line 16)

7. A figure of speech that occurs in lines 16–17 is
   a. transferred epithet
   b. hendiadys
   c. chiasmus
   d. anaphora

8. In line 19, *duci* is
   a. dative
   b. imperative
   c. infinitive
   d. ablative

9. In lines 19–22, we learn that Juno has heard that the descendants of the Trojans
   a. have destroyed Tyre
   b. would destroy Carthage someday
   c. are coming to the haughty king
   d. have helped a king destroy Libya

10. The antecedent of *quae* (line 20) refers to
   a. *progeniem* (line 19)
   b. *sanguine* (line 19)
   c. *duci* (line 19)
   d. *Tyrias* (line 20)

11. *metuens* in line 23 modifies
   a. *id* (line 23)
   b. *memor* (line 23)
   c. *Saturnia* (line 23)
   d. *prima* (line 24)

12. The metrical pattern for the first four feet of line 28 is
   a. dactyl-dactyl-dactyl-spondee
   b. dactyl-spondee-spondee-dactyl
   c. dactyl-spondee-dactyl-spondee
   d. spondee-dactyl-dactyl-spondee

13. *accensa* in line 29 describes

a. the Fates
b. Paris
c. Ganymede
d. Juno

14. In line 30, *reliquias* refers to

a. the Trojan refugees
b. the Greek conquerers
c. the hero Achilles
d. the Latins

15. The clause *multosque per annos/ errabant acti fatis maria omnia circum* (lines 31–32) is best translated

a. and through the years, many wandered, driving the fates around all the seas
b. and driven by the fates, many wandered through the years and the seas around all
c. and driven by the fates they wandered over many years around all the seas
d. and many, through the years, were wandering the seas for the fates around all

Translation *Suggested Time: 10 minutes*

Translate the passage below as literally as possible.

Musa, mihi causas memora, quo numine laeso
quidve dolens regina deum tot volvere casus
insignem pietate virum, tot adire labores
impulerit. Tantaene animis caelestibus irae?

____

____

____

____

____

____

Short Answer Questions

Find, copy out, and provide line references for an example of:

a. metonymy ______________________________

b. transferred epithet (enallage) ______________________________

c. anastrophe ______________________________

d. anaphora ______________________________

Match each of these proper names and adjectives with the best description.

1.	____ Achilles	a.	ancient city on west coast of Italy near the site of future Rome, named for Latinus' daughter
2.	____ Alba Longa	b.	an area of central Italy which includes Rome
3.	____ Danaus	c.	a city on the coast of North Africa
4.	____ Karthago	d.	a region of North Africa
5.	____ Latium	e.	an island where Juno especially was worshipped
6.	____ Lavinium	f.	a city in Phoenicia which established a colony in North Africa
7.	____ Libya	g.	a city in central Italy, considered the mother of Rome, established by Ascanius
8.	____ Parcae	h.	a city in Asia Minor, often associated with Ilium
9.	____ Paris	i.	a name for the Fates, Clotho, Lachesis and Atropos
10.	____ Samos	j.	another name for Juno
11.	____ Saturnia	k.	son of King Priam of Troy, who brought the Spartan queen to Troy
12.	____ Tiberis	l.	anyone from Troy
13.	____ Troia	m.	Greek hero who killed many Trojans; a main character of the *Iliad*
14.	____ Tros	n.	Greek
15.	____ Tyrus	o.	river which runs through Rome to the coast

Essay *Suggested Time: 20 minutes*

In this passage Vergil sets forth some of the themes that he will explore in the rest of the poem: the personal cost of founding Rome, Rome's history, the roles that fate and the gods play, and the powerful force of emotion. In a short, well-organized essay, explain how he establishes these themes.

Support your assertions with references drawn from **throughout** the passage (lines 1–33). All Latin words must be copied or their line numbers provided, AND they must be translated or paraphrased closely enough so that it is clear you understand the Latin. It is your responsibility to convince your reader that you are basing your conclusions on the Latin text and not merely on a general recollection of the passage. Direct your answer to the question; do not merely summarize the passage. Please write your essay on a separate piece of paper.

Scansion

Scan the following lines.

audierat Tyrias olim quae verteret arces (line 20)

errabant acti fatis maria omnia circum (line 32)

LESSON 2: BOOK I. 34–80

Vix e conspectu Siculae telluris in altum
vela dabant laeti et spumas salis aere ruebant,
cum Iuno aeternum servans sub pectore vulnus
haec secum: "Mene incepto desistere victam
nec posse Italia Teucrorum avertere regem!
Quippe vetor fatis. Pallasne exurere classem
Argivum atque ipsos potuit submergere ponto
unius ob noxam et furias Aiacis Oilei?
Ipsa Iovis rapidum iaculata e nubibus ignem
disiecitque rates evertitque aequora ventis,
illum exspirantem transfixo pectore flammas
turbine corripuit scopuloque infixit acuto;
ast ego, quae divum incedo regina Iovisque
et soror et coniunx, una cum gente tot annos
bella gero. Et quisquam numen Iunonis adorat
praeterea aut supplex aris imponet honorem?"
Talia flammato secum dea corde volutans
nimborum in patriam, loca feta furentibus Austris,
Aeoliam venit. Hic vasto rex Aeolus antro
luctantes ventos tempestatesque sonoras
imperio premit ac vinclis et carcere frenat.
Illi indignantes magno cum murmure montis
circum claustra fremunt; celsa sedet Aeolus arce
sceptra tenens mollitque animos et temperat iras.
Ni faciat, maria ac terras caelumque profundum
quippe ferant rapidi secum verrantque per auras;
sed pater omnipotens speluncis abdidit atris
hoc metuens, molemque et montes insuper altos
imposuit, regemque dedit qui foedere certo
et premere et laxas sciret dare iussus habenas.
Ad quem tum Iuno supplex his vocibus usa est:
"Aeole (namque tibi divum pater atque hominum rex
et mulcere dedit fluctus et tollere vento),
gens inimica mihi Tyrrhenum navigat aequor
Ilium in Italiam portans victosque penates:
incute vim ventis submersasque obrue puppes,
aut age diversos et dissice corpora ponto.
Sunt mihi bis septem praestanti corpore Nymphae,
quarum quae forma pulcherrima Deiopea,
conubio iungam stabili propriamque dicabo,
omnes ut tecum meritis pro talibus annos
exigat et pulchra faciat te prole parentem."

Aeolus haec contra: "Tuus, o regina, quid optes
explorare labor; mihi iussa capessere fas est.
Tu mihi, quodcumque hoc regni, tu sceptra Iovemque
concilias, tu das epulis accumbere divum
nimborumque facis tempestatumque potentem."

Comprehension Questions

1. Juno, in her speech to herself (lines 37–49), expresses her feeling that "it isn't fair." What is it that she wants to do but isn't allowed to? Why is she envious of Minerva?

____

____

____

____

____

2. Why did Minerva kill Ajax?

____

____

____

3. How does Vergil explain the natural phenomenon that the winds sometimes blow and sometimes are calm?

____

____

____

4. Vergil uses a metaphor in lines 62–63 to characterize Aeolus' control of the winds. How does this metaphor illuminate the action it describes?

____

____

____

5. Identify two things that Juno promises to Aeolus in her speech. What can you infer about epic values concerning marriage and children from this?

____

____

____

6. Given what you know about the background of the Trojan War, why is Juno's bribe ironic?

____

____

Multiple Choice Questions *Suggested Time: 25 minutes*

1. *vulnus* (line 36) is modified by
   a. *servans* (line 36)
   b. *aeternum* (line 36)
   c. *haec* (line 37)
   d. *pectore* (line 36)

2. *Pallas,* in line 39, is another name for
   a. Juno
   b. Teucer
   c. Minerva
   d. Ajax

3. The case and number of *Argivum* (line 40) is
   a. nominative singular
   b. accusative singular
   c. genitive plural
   d. accusative plural

4. In line 44, *illum* refers to
   a. Jupiter
   b. Ajax
   c. Aeneas
   d. Argivus

5. The metrical pattern of the first four feet of line 49 is
   a. dactyl-dactyl-spondee-spondee
   b. dactyl-spondee-dactyl-spondee
   c. spondee-spondee-dactyl-spondee
   d. dactyl-spondee-spondee-spondee

6. The word *loca* (line 51) is in apposition to
   a. *patriam* (line 51)
   b. *feta* (line 51)
   c. *nimborum* (line 51)
   d. *corde* (line 50)

7. Line 55 contains an example of
   a. chiasmus
   b. alliteration
   c. synchysis
   d. litotes

8. In line 59, *–que* connects
   a. *secum* and *verrant*
   b. *ferant* and *verrant*
   c. *verrant* and *per*
   d. *secum* and *auras*

9. In line 59, *secum* is translated
   a. to himself
   b. with him
   c. to herself
   d. with them

10. The antecedent of *qui* (line 62) is
   a. *regem* (line 62)
   b. *montes* (line 61)
   c. *foedere* (line 62)
   d. *iussus* (line 63)

11. The phrase *divum . . . rex* (line 65) refers to
   a. Aiax
   b. Priamus
   c. Aeneas
   d. Jupiter

12. The case and number of *fluctus* (line 66) is
   a. nominative singular
   b. accusative plural
   c. nominative plural
   d. genitive singular

13. In line 67, the phrase *gens inimica mihi* describes
   a. Trojans
   b. Greeks
   c. Nymphae
   d. Danai

14. From line 68, we learn that
   a. Penates is bringing Ilium into Italy
   b. the remnants of the Trojan state and its religion are being brought to Italy
   c. Ilium conquered the Penates as they were being carried to Italy
   d. the defeated Trojans are carrying the Penates into Ilium

15. In line 70, *dissice* is
   a. present infinitive
   b. accusative singular
   c. present imperative
   d. ablative singular

16. Why is Deiopea an especially valuable bribe?
   a. she is the most beautiful
   b. she has beautiful offspring
   c. she is fourteen years old
   d. she has performed many duties for Juno

17. The form *iungam* (line 73) is a(n)
   a. perfect participle
   b. present subjunctive
   c. accusative singular
   d. future indicative

18. Line 76 contains
   a. an indirect question
   b. an indirect statement
   c. a relative clause of purpose
   d. an indirect command

19. Lines 78–79 contain the rhetorical device
    a. transferred epithet
    b. chiasmus
    c. metaphor
    d. anaphora

20. In lines 78–80, Aeolus says that he will fulfill Juno's request because
    a. he wants Jupiter's scepter
    b. she has offered him an outstanding bribe
    c. she has given him whatever power he has
    d. he prefers the gods' feasts to having power

Translation *Suggested time: 15 minutes*

Translate the passage below as literally as possible.

Ipsa Iovis rapidum iaculata e nubibus ignem
disiecitque rates evertitque aequora ventis,
illum exspirantem transfixo pectore flammas
turbine corripuit scopuloque infixit acuto;
ast ego, quae divum incedo regina Iovisque
et soror et coniunx, una cum gente tot annos
bella gero.

____

____

____

____

____

____

____

Short Answer Questions

From lines 34–64 , find, copy out, and provide line references for:

1. a second declension genitive plural in *–um* ______________________
2. an ablative of separation ______________________
3. an appositive ______________________
4. three verbs in the subjunctive ______________________
5. three participles NOT in the nominative ______________________

6. the objects of these participles:

   servans (line 36) ______________________

   exspirantem (line 44) ______________________

   volutans (line 50) ______________________

   tenens (line 57) ______________________

   metuens (line 61) ______________________

7. an example of metonymy ______________________

8. a metaphor ______________________

9. an example of hendiadys ______________________

From lines 65–80, find, copy out, and provide line references for:

10. two verbs in the future tense ______________________

11. an example of prolepsis ______________________

12. a dative of possession ______________________

13. a second declension genitive plural in *–um* ______________________

14. an example of anaphora ______________________

15. two vocatives ______________________

16. four imperatives ______________________

17. a superlative adjective ______________________

18. an indirect question ______________________

19. an example of alliteration ______________________

Who or what are the following?

1. Sicilia ______________________

2. Pallas ______________________

3. Aiax Oileus ______________________

4. Aeolus ______________________

Essay *Suggested Time: 20 minutes*

What can we learn about Juno's character from her speech to Aeolus in lines 65–75? Present your response in a well-organized essay.

Support your assertions with references drawn from **throughout** this passage (lines 65–75 only). All Latin words must be copied or their line numbers provided, AND they must be translated or paraphrased closely enough so that it is clear you understand the Latin. It is your responsibility to convince your reader that you are basing your conclusions on the Latin text and not merely on a general recollection of the passage. Direct your answer to the question; do not merely summarize the passage. Please write your essay on a separate piece of paper.

Scansion

Scan the following lines.

quippe vetor fatis. Pallasne exurere classem

Argivum atque ipsos potuit submergere ponto

(lines 39–40)

illum exspirantem transfixo pectore flammas (line 44)

ast ego, quae divum incedo regina, Iovisque (line 46)

And a harder one:

unius ob noxam et furias Aiacis Oilei (line 41)

LESSON 3: BOOK I. 81–131

Haec ubi dicta, cavum conversa cuspide montem
impulit in latus: ac venti, velut agmine facto,
qua data porta, ruunt et terras turbine perflant.
Incubuere mari, totumque a sedibus imis
una Eurusque Notusque ruunt creberque procellis
Africus, et vastos volvunt ad litora fluctus.
Insequitur clamorque virum stridorque rudentum;
eripiunt subito nubes caelumque diemque
Teucrorum ex oculis; ponto nox incubat atra;
intonuere poli, et crebris micat ignibus aether
praesentemque viris intentant omnia mortem.
Extemplo Aeneae solvuntur frigore membra;
ingemit et duplices tendens ad sidera palmas
talia voce refert: "O terque quaterque beati,
quis ante ora patrum Troiae sub moenibus altis
contigit oppetere! O Danaum fortissime gentis
Tydide! Mene Iliacis occumbere campis
non potuisse tuaque animam hanc effundere dextra,
saevus ubi Aeacidae telo iacet Hector, ubi ingens
Sarpedon, ubi tot Simois correpta sub undis
scuta virum galeasque et fortia corpora volvit!"
Talia iactanti stridens Aquilone procella
velum adversa ferit, fluctusque ad sidera tollit.
franguntur remi; tum prora avertit et undis
dat latus, insequitur cumulo praeruptus aquae mons.
Hi summo in fluctu pendent; his unda dehiscens
terram inter fluctus aperit; furit aestus harenis.
Tres Notus abreptas in saxa latentia torquet
(saxa vocant Itali mediis quae in fluctibus Aras,
dorsum immane mari summo), tres Eurus ab alto
in brevia et Syrtes urget, miserabile visu,
inliditque vadis atque aggere cingit harenae.
Unam, quae Lycios fidumque vehebat Oronten,
ipsius ante oculos ingens a vertice pontus
in puppim ferit: excutitur pronusque magister
volvitur in caput, ast illam ter fluctus ibidem
torquet agens circum et rapidus vorat aequore vertex.
Apparent rari nantes in gurgite vasto,
arma virum tabulaeque et Troia gaza per undas.
Iam validam Ilionei navem, iam fortis Achatae,
et qua vectus Abas, et qua grandaevus Aletes,
vicit hiems; laxis laterum compagibus omnes
accipiunt inimicum imbrem rimisque fatiscunt.

Interea magno misceri murmure pontum
emissamque hiemem sensit Neptunus et imis
stagna refusa vadis, graviter commotus, et alto
prospiciens summa placidum caput extulit unda.
Disiectam Aeneae toto videt aequore classem,
fluctibus oppressos Troas caelique ruina;
nec latuere doli fratrem Iunonis et irae.
Eurum ad se Zephyrumque vocat, dehinc talia fatur:

Comprehension Questions

1. In the simile in lines 82–83, to what are the rushing winds compared?

2. In line 97, Vergil uses a patronymic ("son of...") to refer to an important character, Tydides (lit., "son of Tydeus"). Tydides is the patronymic for whom? Why would Aeneas mention him here?

3. For whom is Aeacides the patronymic?

4. To what event is Aeneas referring in line 99?

5. Lines 103 and 105 each contain an example of hyperbole. Give one word from each line that best represents this, and explain the effect of each hyperbole.

6. Vergil mentions five ships specifically that were damaged by the storm. With what comrade was each associated?

7. Line 124 contains a verbal echo of a line of the earlier passage in which Aeolus' control of the wind is described. Identify which line.

8. Why is Neptune upset?

9. Who does he know has caused the storm?

Short Answer Questions

Indicate True or False.

1. ____ In line 84, *incubuere* is an infinitive.
2. ____ *ruunt* (line 85) has three subjects.
3. ____ Line 87 describes the sounds of the setting.
4. ____ In line 92, *extemplo* is dative.
5. ____ Aeneas in his speech of lines 94–101 wishes that he were dead.
6. ____ Simois killed Sarpedon.
7. ____ The subject of *dat* (line 105) is *latus.*
8. ____ In line 110, *dorsum immane* is in apposition to *Aras* (line 109).
9. ____ *visu* (line 111) is a perfect participle.
10. ____ *ipsius* (line 114) refers to *Oronten* (line 113).
11. ____ In lines 115–16, we learn that a ship's pilot is struck because of the storm.
12. ____ Line 118 can be translated "There appear scattered men floating in the huge whirlpool."
13. ____ The object of *vicit* in line 122 is *hiems.*
14. ____ In line 122, *laterum* is accusative.
15. ____ *sensit* (line 125) governs an indirect statement with three accusative subjects + infinitives.
16. ____ *commotus* (line 126) and *prospiciens* (line 127) both modify *Neptunus.*
17. ____ Line 128 can be translated "Aeneas sees his fleet scattered on the sea."
18. ____ Line 129 contains hyperbole.
19. ____ In line 130, *latuere* is perfect indicative.
20. ____ We learn that Neptune is angry in line 130.
21. ____ Line 131 contains synizesis.

Copy out an example of each of these figures of speech and provide a line reference in parentheses. (There are several examples of some of these in the passage.)

a. apostrophe ______________________________

b. hysteron proteron ______________________________

c. anaphora (find at least three examples of this) ______________________________

____

____

d. alliteration____

e. polysyndeton ____

f. onomatopoeia____

g. hyperbole ____

Put the following into one of the categories listed below. (Some names appear in earlier lines.)

Achates	Achilles	Aeolia	Africus	Aias
Aquilo	Arae	Auster	Diomedes	Eurus
Hector	Ilioneus	Lavinium	Libya	Notus
Orontes	Paris	Priam	Sarpedon	Simois
Tiberis	Tyrrhenia	Zephyrus		

Greek heroes/allies____

____

Trojan heroes/allies ____

____

Winds____

____

Places ____

____

Translation *Suggested time: 15 minutes*

Translate the following lines as literally as possible.

Interea magno misceri murmure pontum
emissamque hiemem sensit Neptunus et imis
stagna refusa vadis, graviter commotus, et alto
prospiciens summa placidum caput extulit unda.
Disiectam Aeneae toto videt aequore classem,
fluctibus oppressos Troas caelique ruina;
nec latuere doli fratrem Iunonis et irae.

____

____

____

____

____

____

____

Essays *Suggested time: 40 minutes (20 minutes per essay)*

1. In lines 81–91, Vergil establishes a vivid and violent setting for the events that follow. In a short, well-organized essay, explain how he creates this setting.

2. The first appearance of Aeneas in the poem occurs in lines 92–101. In a short, well-organized essay, describe how Vergil characterizes Aeneas in this passage.

For each essay above, support your assertions with references drawn from **throughout** the passage indicated by each essay, i.e., lines 81–91 only for essay #1 and lines 92–101 only for essay #2. All Latin words must be copied or their line numbers provided, AND they must be translated or paraphrased closely enough so that it is clear you understand the Latin. It is your responsibility to convince your reader that you are basing your conclusions on the Latin text and not merely on a general recollection of the passage. Direct your answer to the question; do not merely summarize the passage. Please write your essays on a separate piece of paper.

Scansion

Scan the following lines.

hi summo in fluctu pendent; his unda dehiscens

terram inter fluctus aperit; furit aestus harenis.

tres Notus abreptas in saxa latentia torquet

(saxa vocant Itali mediis quae in fluctibus Aras,

dorsum immane mari summo), tres Eurus ab alto

(lines 106–110)

A bit trickier:

iam validam Ilionei navem, iam fortis Achatae (line 120)

LESSON 4: BOOK I. 132–179

"Tantane vos generis tenuit fiducia vestri?
Iam caelum terramque meo sine numine, venti,
miscere et tantas audetis tollere moles?
Quos ego—sed motos praestat componere fluctus.
Post mihi non simili poena commissa luetis.
Maturate fugam regique haec dicite vestro:
non illi imperium pelagi saevumque tridentem,
sed mihi sorte datum. Tenet ille immania saxa,
vestras, Eure, domos; illa se iactet in aula
Aeolus et clauso ventorum carcere regnet."
Sic ait, et dicto citius tumida aequora placat
collectasque fugat nubes solemque reducit.
Cymothoe simul et Triton adnixus acuto
detrudunt naves scopulo; levat ipse tridenti
et vastas aperit Syrtes et temperat aequor
atque rotis summas levibus perlabitur undas.
Ac veluti magno in populo cum saepe coorta est
seditio saevitque animis ignobile vulgus
iamque faces et saxa volant, furor arma ministrat;
tum, pietate gravem ac meritis si forte virum quem
conspexere, silent arrectisque auribus astant;
ille regit dictis animos et pectora mulcet:
sic cunctus pelagi cecidit fragor, aequora postquam
prospiciens genitor caeloque invectus aperto
flectit equos curruque volans dat lora secundo.
Defessi Aeneadae quae proxima litora cursu
contendunt petere, et Libyae vertuntur ad oras.
Est in secessu longo locus: insula portum
efficit obiectu laterum, quibus omnis ab alto
frangitur inque sinus scindit sese unda reductos.
Hinc atque hinc vastae rupes geminique minantur
in caelum scopuli, quorum sub vertice late
aequora tuta silent; tum silvis scaena coruscis
desuper, horrentique atrum nemus imminet umbra.
Fronte sub adversa scopulis pendentibus antrum;
intus aquae dulces vivoque sedilia saxo,
Nympharum domus. Hic fessas non vincula naves
ulla tenent, unco non alligat ancora morsu.
Huc septem Aeneas collectis navibus omni
ex numero subit, ac magno telluris amore
egressi optata potiuntur Troes harena
et sale tabentis artus in litore ponunt.

Ac primum silici scintillam excudit Achates
suscepitque ignem foliis atque arida circum
nutrimenta dedit rapuitque in fomite flammam.
Tum Cererem corruptam undis Cerealiaque arma
expediunt fessi rerum, frugesque receptas
et torrere parant flammis et frangere saxo.

Comprehension Questions

1. How is Neptune's mood illustrated in lines 132–41? Provide line references in parentheses for any Latin you cite.

2. How does Neptune defend his sphere of influence?

3. Who are Cymothoe and Triton?

4. What action in the narrative is enhanced by the simile (lines 148–153)?

5. Why do Aeneas and his followers beach their ships where they do?

6. In the ecphrasis (lines 159–69), Vergil uses language that suggests both a peaceful and a threatening atmosphere. Which words (with their line numbers) connote peacefulness and which a threat?

7. What does the phrase *magno telluris amore* (line 171) tell us about the shipwrecked Trojans?

8. Why do Achates' actions in lines 174–76 receive so much emphasis from Vergil? ______________

____

____

9. Why does Vergil remind the reader of the importance of fire and the preparation of food at this point in the plot? ______________

____

____

Multiple Choice Questions *Suggested time: 18 minutes*

1. *domos* (line 140) is in apposition to
   a. *immania* (line 139)
   b. *vestras* (line 140)
   c. *Eure* (line 140)
   d. *saxa* (line 139)

2. The tense and mood of *iactet* (line 140) is
   a. present indicative
   b. present subjunctive
   c. future indicative
   d. perfect subjunctive

3. The form of *citius* (line 142) is
   a. comparative adjective
   b. comparative adverb
   c. positive adverb
   d. positive adjective

4. The best translation of lines 142–43 (*Sic . . . reducit*) is
   a. Thus he speaks, and more quickly than a word he calms the swollen seas and puts to flight the gathered clouds and brings back the sun.
   b. Thus he speaks, and with his rather quick word he calms the swollen seas and sends off the collected clouds and leads back the sun.
   c. He speaks thus, and with his speech he calms the swift, swelling seas and sends away the collected clouds and leads back the sun.
   d. He speaks thus, and he placates the swollen seas with his swift word and puts to flight the gathered clouds and brings back the sun.

5. The case and number of *vulgus* (line 149) is
   a. accusative plural
   b. nominative singular
   c. accusative singular
   d. nominative plural

6. Vergil makes the point in line 150 that
   a. only crazy people will throw weapons in a crowd
   b. people will throw torches if they are ignoble
   c. weapons increase the anger of a crowd
   d. when a mob is angry, it will use anything as a weapon

7. In line 153, *ille* refers to
   a. *virum* (line 151)
   b. *pietate* (line 151)
   c. Triton (understood)
   d. *fragor* (line 154)

8. The *–que* in line 155 connects
   a. *genitor* and *invectus*
   b. *prospiciens* and *flectit*
   c. *caelo* and *aperto*
   d. *prospiciens* and *invectus*

9. The case of *curru* (line 156) is
   a. ablative
   b. nominative
   c. dative
   d. accusative

10. The best translation of lines 157–58 (*Defessi . . . oras*) is
   a. Aeneas' tired followers strive toward the shores in their course, which is very near, and they are turned toward Libya's coast.
   b. Aeneas' tired followers, who are nearest to the shore in their course, aim toward it, and they are turned toward Libya's coast.
   c. The weary followers of Aeneas strive to seek with their course the shores which are nearest, and they are turned toward the coast of Libya.
   d. The weary followers of Aeneas seek in their haste the nearest shores, which they strive toward, and they are turned toward the coast of Libya.

11. The antecedent of *quibus* (line 160) is
   a. *laterum* (line 160)
   b. *obiectu* (line 160)
   c. *omnis* (line 160)
   d. *sinus* (line 161)

12. The case and number of *sinus* (line 161) is
   a. nominative singular
   b. genitive singular
   c. nominative plural
   d. accusative plural

13. The metrical pattern of the first four feet of line 162 is
   a. dactyl-dactyl-dactyl-spondee
   b. dactyl-spondee-spondee-spondee
   c. spondee-spondee-spondee-dactyl
   d. spondee-dactyl-spondee-dactyl

14. In line 170, *omni* modifies
   a. *huc* (line 170)
   b. *septem* (line 170)
   c. *numero* (line 171)
   d. *amore* (line 171)

15. A figure of speech that occurs in line 177 is
   a. personification
   b. anaphora
   c. aposiopesis
   d. metonymy

Translation *Suggested time: 20 minutes*

Translate the following lines as literally as possible.

Huc septem Aeneas collectis navibus omni
ex numero subit, ac magno telluris amore
egressi optata potiuntur Troes harena
et sale tabentis artus in litore ponunt.
Ac primum silici scintillam excudit Achates
suscepitque ignem foliis atque arida circum
nutrimenta dedit rapuitque in fomite flammam.

____

____

____

____

____

____

____

Short Answer Questions

Each of these lines contains at least one figure of speech. Identify one figure of speech in each line.

1. *Post mihi non simili poena commissa luetis* ______________________________
2. *conspexere, silent arrectisque auribus astant* ______________________________
3. *frangitur inque sinus scindit sese unda reductos* ______________________________
4. *Nympharum domus. Hic fessas non vincula naves* ______________________________
5. *tum Cererem corruptam undis Cerealiaque arma* ______________________________

Essay *Suggested time: 20 minutes*

In his simile in lines 148–53, whom is Vergil describing? To whom else may he be referring (consider line 10 of the poem)? From your knowledge of Roman history, why might this simile particularly resonate with a Roman reader? Present your response in a well-organized essay.

Support your assertions with references drawn from **throughout** this passage (lines 148–53 only). All Latin words must be copied or their line numbers provided, AND they must be translated or paraphrased closely enough so that it is clear you understand the Latin. It is your responsibility to convince your reader that you are basing your conclusions on the Latin text and not merely on a general recollection of the passage. Direct your answer to the question; do not merely summarize the passage. Please write your essay on a separate piece of paper.

Scansion

Scan the following lines.

ac primum silici scintillam excudit Achates

suscepitque ignem foliis atque arida circum

nutrimenta dedit rapuitque in fomite flammam.

tum Cererem corruptam undis Cerealiaque arma

(lines 174–177)

LESSON 5: BOOK I. 180–222

Aeneas scopulum interea conscendit, et omnem
prospectum late pelago petit, Anthea si quem
iactatum vento videat Phrygiasque biremes
aut Capyn aut celsis in puppibus arma Caici.
Navem in conspectu nullam, tres litore cervos
prospicit errantes; hos tota armenta sequuntur
a tergo et longum per valles pascitur agmen.
Constitit hic arcumque manu celeresque sagittas
corripuit fidus quae tela gerebat Achates,
ductoresque ipsos primum capita alta ferentes
cornibus arboreis sternit, tum vulgus et omnem
miscet agens telis nemora inter frondea turbam;
nec prius absistit quam septem ingentia victor
corpora fundat humi et numerum cum navibus aequet;
hinc portum petit et socios partitur in omnes.
Vina bonus quae deinde cadis onerarat Acestes
litore Trinacrio dederatque abeuntibus heros
dividit, et dictis maerentia pectora mulcet:
"O socii (neque enim ignari sumus ante malorum),
o passi graviora, dabit deus his quoque finem.
Vos et Scyllaeam rabiem penitusque sonantes
accestis scopulos, vos et Cyclopia saxa
experti: revocate animos maestumque timorem
mittite; forsan et haec olim meminisse iuvabit.
Per varios casus, per tot discrimina rerum
tendimus in Latium, sedes ubi fata quietas
ostendunt; illic fas regna resurgere Troiae.
Durate, et vosmet rebus servate secundis."
Talia voce refert curisque ingentibus aeger
spem vultu simulat, premit altum corde dolorem.
Illi se praedae accingunt dapibusque futuris:
tergora diripiunt costis et viscera nudant;
pars in frusta secant veribusque trementia figunt,
litore aëna locant alii flammasque ministrant.
Tum victu revocant vires, fusique per herbam
implentur veteris Bacchi pinguisque ferinae.
Postquam exempta fames epulis mensaeque remotae,
amissos longo socios sermone requirunt,
spemque metumque inter dubii, seu vivere credant,
sive extrema pati nec iam exaudire vocatos.
Praecipue pius Aeneas nunc acris Oronti,
nunc Amyci casum gemit et crudelia secum
fata Lyci fortemque Gyan fortemque Cloanthum.

Comprehension Questions

1. How many ships survive the storm? ____________________
2. Which eight lost comrades are mentioned by name? ____________________

   ____
3. How does Aeneas demonstrate concern for his men? ____________________
4. Where is Phrygia? ____________________
5. Where is the *litus Trinacrium*? ____________________
6. Where is Latium? ____________________
7. In lines 184–94, what words suggest that a military metaphor is being employed?

   ____

   ____

   ____
8. In line 197, Vergil uses the phrase *pectora mulcet.* He used the same phrase, in the same position in the line, in line 153. What implicit comparison does he expect the reader to make?

   ____

   ____

   ____

   ____
9. What other epic hero and his followers encountered Scylla and the Cyclops? ____________________
10. In his speech, Aeneas encourages his men by referring to the past and to the future. How does he recollect the past? What events in the future does he choose to speak about in hopes of buoying up his comrades' spirits? How does he himself feel about what he's saying? Cite specific Latin words or phrases with line numbers to support your answers.

    ____

    ____

    ____

    ____

    ____

    ____

    ____

    ____

    ____

11. What specific phrases in Aeneas' speech suggest the theme of Rome's establishment?

____

12. After the men have eaten, what do they do? What is their state of mind? Make sure you cite and translate specific words and phrases to support your answer.

____

____

____

____

____

____

____

____

____

____

____

Short Answer Questions

Choose the better translation.

1. *navem in conspectu nullam, tres litore cervos/ prospicit errantes* (lines 184–185)
   a. he sees no ship in sight, but three stags wandering on the shore
   b. no ship is in sight, but he catches sight of stags wandering on the shore in three places

2. *nec prius absistit quam septem ingentia victor/ corpora fundat humi et numerum cum navibus aequet* (lines 192–193)
   a. nor does he stop earlier, and the huge victor lays low the seven bodies which were on the ground, and he equals the number with the ships
   b. nor does he stop before, as victor, he lays low seven huge bodies onto the ground and makes equal their number with the ships

3. *vina bonus quae deinde cadis onerarat Acestes/ litore Trinacrio dederatque abeuntibus heros/dividit* (lines 195–196)
   a. the wines which good Acestes then had loaded in jars the hero divides on the Sicilian shore and gives to them as they depart
   b. he divides the wine which the good hero Acestes had then loaded into jars on the Sicilian shore and had given to them as they departed

4. *illi se praedae accingunt dapibusque futuris:/ tergora diripiunt costis et viscera nudant* (lines 210–211)
   a. they gird themselves for the prey and the feasts about to be: they tear the hide from the ribs and lay bare the vitals
   b. they themselves gird the prey for future feasts: they tear the hide and bare the ribs and vitals

5. *tum victu revocant vires, fusique per herbam/ implentur veteris Bacchi pinguisque ferinae* (lines 214–215)
   a. then they recall the men with food, and through the grass they are filled with the old wine poured out and with the rich game
   b. then they recall their strength with food, and poured out through the grass they are filled with old wine and rich game

What figure of speech occurs in each of the following lines?

1. *navem in conspectu nullam, tres litore cervos* (line 184)
   a. zeugma
   b. metonymy
   c. asyndeton
   d. enallage

2. *vina bonus quae deinde cadis onerarat Acestes/ litore Trinacrio dederatque abeuntibus heros/ dividit* (lines 195–197)
   a. personification
   b. synchysis
   c. chiasmus
   d. hyperbaton

3. *spem vultu simulat, premit altum corde dolorem* (line 209)
   a. anaphora
   b. chiasmus
   c. prolepsis
   d. synecdoche

4. *implentur veteris Bacchi pinguisque ferinae* (line 215)
   a. tmesis
   b. metonymy
   c. litotes
   d. onomatopoeia

5. *amissos longo socios sermone requirunt* (line 217)
   a. synchysis
   b. chiasmus
   c. simile
   d. hendiadys

6. *spemque metumque inter dubii, seu vivere credant* (line 218)
   a. pleonasm
   b. hyperbole
   c. anastrophe
   d. alliteration

What noun does each of these adjectives/participles modify?

a. *iactatum* (line 182) ____________________

b. *tres* (line 184) ____________________

c. *errantes* (line 185) ____________________

d. *celeres* (line 187) ____________________

e. *ferentes* (line 189) ____________________

f. *ingentia* (line 192) ____________________

g. *omnes* (line 194) ____________________

h. *bonus* (line 195) ____________________

i. *passi* (line 199) ____________________

j. *sonantes* (line 200) ____________________

k. *quietas* (line 205) ____________________

l. *pinguis* (line 215) ____________________

m. *longo* (line 217) ____________________

n. *crudelia* (line 221) ____________________

What two items does each –*que* connect?

a. line 187 (first –*que*) ____________________ and ____________________

b. line 187 (second –*que*) ____________________ and ____________________

c. line 189 ____________________ and ____________________

d. line 208 ____________________ and ____________________

e. line 212 ____________________ and ____________________

f. line 213 ____________________ and ____________________

g. line 214 ____________________ and ____________________

h. line 215 ____________________ and ____________________

What is the object(s) of these verbs/participles?

a. *sequuntur* (line 185) ____________________

b. *ferentes* (line 189) ____________________

c. *dederat* (line 196) ____________________

d. *passi* (line 199) ____________________

e. *refert* (line 208) ____________________

f. *accingunt* (line 210) ____________________

g. *figunt* (line 212) ____________________

h. *gemit* (line 221) ____________________

Translation *Suggested time: 15 minutes*

Translate the following lines as literally as possible.

"O socii (neque enim ignari sumus ante malorum),
o passi graviora, dabit deus his quoque finem.
Vos et Scyllaeam rabiem penitusque sonantes
accestis scopulos, vos et Cyclopia saxa
experti: revocate animos maestumque timorem
mittite; forsan et haec olim meminisse iuvabit.

____

____

____

____

____

____

Essay *Suggested time: 20 minutes*

This passage recalls several episodes in the *Odyssey*: Odysseus killing a deer for his men, his encounters with Scylla and the Cyclops, and the detailed description of the preparation of food. Given these epic allusions, Aeneas' brief "private moment" in lines 208–9 stands out. Why does Vergil show Aeneas as having these two facets, the heroic and the human? Present your response in a well-organized essay.

Support your assertions with references drawn from **throughout** this passage (lines 180–222). All Latin words must be copied or their line numbers provided, AND they must be translated or paraphrased closely enough so that it is clear you understand the Latin. It is your responsibility to convince your reader that you are basing your conclusions on the Latin text and not merely on a general recollection of the passage. Direct your answer to the question; do not merely summarize the passage. Please write your essay on a separate piece of paper.

Scansion

Scan the following lines.

vina bonus quae deinde cadis onerarat Acestes

litore Trinacrio dederatque abeuntibus heros

dividit, et dictis maerentia pectora mulcet:

"O socii (neque enim ignari sumus ante malorum),

(lines 195–198)

Notes

LESSON 6: BOOK I. 223–277

Et iam finis erat, cum Iuppiter aethere summo
despiciens mare velivolum terrasque iacentes
litoraque et latos populos, sic vertice caeli
constitit et Libyae defixit lumina regnis.
Atque illum tales iactantem pectore curas
tristior et lacrimis oculos suffusa nitentes
adloquitur Venus: "O qui res hominumque deumque
aeternis regis imperiis et fulmine terres,
quid meus Aeneas in te committere tantum,
quid Troes potuere, quibus tot funera passis
cunctus ob Italiam terrarum clauditur orbis?
Certe hinc Romanos olim volventibus annis,
hinc fore ductores, revocato a sanguine Teucri,
qui mare, qui terras omnes dicione tenerent,
pollicitus—quae te, genitor, sententia vertit?
Hoc equidem occasum Troiae tristesque ruinas
solabar fatis contraria fata rependens;
nunc eadem fortuna viros tot casibus actos
insequitur. Quem das finem, rex magne, laborum?
Antenor potuit mediis elapsus Achivis
Illyricos penetrare sinus atque intima tutus
regna Liburnorum et fontem superare Timavi,
unde per ora novem vasto cum murmure montis
it mare proruptum et pelago premit arva sonanti.
Hic tamen ille urbem Patavi sedesque locavit
Teucrorum et genti nomen dedit armaque fixit
Troia, nunc placida compostus pace quiescit:
nos, tua progenies, caeli quibus adnuis arcem,
navibus (infandum!) amissis unius ob iram
prodimur atque Italis longe disiungimur oris.
Hic pietatis honos? Sic nos in sceptra reponis?"
Olli subridens hominum sator atque deorum
vultu, quo caelum tempestatesque serenat,
oscula libavit natae, dehinc talia fatur:
"Parce metu, Cytherea, manent immota tuorum
fata tibi; cernes urbem et promissa Lavini
moenia, sublimemque feres ad sidera caeli
magnanimum Aenean; neque me sententia vertit.
Hic tibi (fabor enim, quando haec te cura remordet,
longius et volvens fatorum arcana movebo)
bellum ingens geret Italia populosque feroces
contundet moresque viris et moenia ponet,
tertia dum Latio regnantem viderit aestas,

ternaque transierint Rutulis hiberna subactis.
At puer Ascanius, cui nunc cognomen Iulo
additur (Ilus erat, dum res stetit Ilia regno),
triginta magnos volvendis mensibus orbes
imperio explebit, regnumque ab sede Lavini
transferet, et Longam multa vi muniet Albam.
Hic iam ter centum totos regnabitur annos
gente sub Hectorea, donec regina sacerdos
Marte gravis geminam partu dabit Ilia prolem.
Inde lupae fulvo nutricis tegmine laetus
Romulus excipiet gentem et Mavortia condet
moenia Romanosque suo de nomine dicet.

Comprehension Questions

1. In lines 223–26, Jupiter makes his first appearance. Where is he? What does he see? Imagine a movie shot from his perspective; what would the shot look like? ______________________

____

____

____

____

2. What is Venus' mood? What words or phrases support this? Translate the words or phrases that you choose. ____

____

____

____

3. Some people have described Venus as "whiny" in this speech. How could someone make this inference based on lines 231–39? ____

____

____

____

4. The question Venus asks in line 241 recalls what other line that you have already read? What might Vergil mean to suggest with this echo?

____

____

____

____

5. Why does Venus think that it is unfair that Antenor has safely escaped the Greeks and the Illyrians and has established Padua when Aeneas is still unsettled? ____________________

____

____

____

6. The word *pietatis* occurs in line 253. Where else have you seen references to *pietas*? To whose *pietas* is Venus referring here? ____________________

____

____

____

7. How is Jupiter's attitude toward his daughter described? ____________________

____

____

____

8. In Jupiter's prophecy to Venus about Rome, how many years will it be between the time Aeneas conquers the Rutulians and Romulus is born? ____________________

9. In lines 261–77, Jupiter consoles Venus by giving her a preview of four stages of Rome's early history. For each of these stages, copy out and and translate a phrase that summarizes it.

____

____

____

____

10. Vergil draws attention here to two different myths about Rome's foundation. How can the city trace its ancestry to both Venus, goddess of love, and Mars, god of war?

____

____

____

____

11. Jupiter says that the Romans will not be called by a name that refers to their Trojan past. How did the Romans get their name? ______

12. In this passage there are many words that are related to the idea of having power. Copy out and give line numbers for at least twelve. (There are nine from the *reg-* stem alone.) What point do you think Vergil is trying to make by using such language?

13. Jupiter gives a detailed account of Aeneas' and Rome's future. Who establishes Rome?

14. Vergil has Jupiter use the phrase *geminam prolem* to describe the offspring of *Ilia.* Why does he then go on to give details about Romulus only? ______

Multiple Choice Questions *Suggested time: 25 minutes*

1. In line 223, *Et iam finis erat,* in this context, refers to
   a. the end of the storm
   b. the end of the day
   c. the edge of the Libyan territory
   d. the territory where Jupiter is

2. In line 226,
   a. the Libyans look at their kingdom
   b. Jupiter gives light to the kingdom of Libya
   c. the Libyan kingdom is illuminated
   d. Jupiter looks at Libya

3. From lines 227–29 we learn that Jupiter
   a. has worries
   b. is rather sad
   c. is weeping
   d. has shining eyes

4. In line 228, *nitentes* modifies
   a. *lacrimis* (line 228)
   b. *suffusa* (line 228)
   c. *curas* (line 227)
   d. *oculos* (line 228)

5. In line 230, *regis* is
   a. future indicative
   b. genitive singular
   c. present indicative
   d. ablative plural

6. The best translation of lines 232–233 (*quibus . . . orbis*) is
   a. for whom, with so many deaths having been endured, all the globe of the earth is shut off on account of Italy
   b. to whom, having endured so many deaths, all the globe of the earth is shut off on account of Italy
   c. for these, with so many deaths having been suffered, all the globe of the earth is shut off from Italy
   d. to these, having suffered so many deaths, the whole globe is shut off on account of the lands of Italy

7. Teucer (*Teucri,* line 235) is
   a. one of Troy's earliest kings
   b. one of Rome's earliest kings
   c. a Roman leader
   d. one of Aeneas' descendants

8. Lines 245–46 (*unde . . . sonanti*) are best translated
   a. from where through nine mouths with a vast roar of the mountain it goes to the furious sea and the resounding flood overwhelms the fields
   b. whence through nine vast mouths with a murmur of the mountain it goes to the furious sea and it presses the land with a resounding flood
   c. from where, through its new openings, with a vast murmur of a mountain the furious sea goes and presses the land with the sounding water
   d. whence through nine mouths with a huge roar of a mountain it goes as a furious sea and overwhelms the fields with its resounding flood

9. In line 247, *ille* refers to
   a. Teucer
   b. Patavus
   c. Antenor
   d. Timavus

10. The *iram* (line 251) belongs to
   a. Juno
   b. Teucer
   c. Cytherea
   d. Aeneas

11. The metrical pattern of the first four feet of line 251 is
    a. dactyl-dactyl-spondee-spondee
    b. dactyl-spondee-dactyl-spondee
    c. dactyl-dactyl-spondee-dactyl
    d. dactyl-spondee-spondee-spondee

12. The form of *feres* (line 259) is
    a. future indicative
    b. present subjunctive
    c. present indicative
    d. imperfect subjunctive

13. The meaning of *quando* in line 261 is
    a. then
    b. whenever
    c. when
    d. since

14. In line 264, Jupiter says that
    a. Italy will place customs and walls upon men
    b. Aeneas will establish customs and build walls
    c. Italy will establish strength and walls (in its empire)
    d. Aeneas will place his strength in building walls

15. In line 264, *viris* is
    a. genitive singular
    b. dative plural
    c. accusative plural
    d. ablative plural

16. Line 264 contains the figure of speech
    a. litotes
    b. synchysis
    c. hendiadys
    d. alliteration

17. In line 265, *dum* means
    a. then
    b. while
    c. until
    d. when

18. Lines 267–68 are important because they explain
    a. how Ascanius was in Ilium as a boy
    b. how the Ilium kingdom was ruled by Ilus
    c. Ascanius' lineage
    d. how Iulus is derived from Ilium

19. In line 273, *gente Hectorea* refers to the
    a. Rutulians
    b. Lavinians
    c. Romans
    d. Trojans

20. In line 274, *gravis* means
    a. pregnant
    b. serious
    c. heavy
    d. grave

Translation *Suggested time: 20 minutes*

Translate the following passage as literally as possible.

quid meus Aeneas in te committere tantum,
quid Troes potuere, quibus tot funera passis
cunctus ob Italiam terrarum clauditur orbis?
Certe hinc Romanos olim volventibus annis,
hinc fore ductores, revocato a sanguine Teucri,
qui mare, qui terras omnes dicione tenerent,
pollicitus—quae te, genitor, sententia vertit?

____

____

____

____

____

____

____

Short Answer Questions

1. Copy out two lines that contain alliteration. Provide the line reference in parentheses for your choice.

   ____

   ____

2. Copy out a line that contains synchysis. Provide the line reference in parentheses for your choice.

   ____

3. What use of the accusative is *oculos* (line 228)? ______________________

4. *Aeneas* (line 231) is the subject of what verb? ______________________

5. Line 236 has language that echoes what earlier line in the passage? ______________________

6. What phrase from lines 229–41 focuses on the passage of time? ______________________

   ____

7. What case and number is *sinus* (line 243)? ______________________

8. What part of speech is *hic* (line 247)? ______________________________

9. What is the antecedent of *quo* (line 255)? ______________________________

10. Who or what is *Cytherea* (line 257)? ______________________________

11. Lines 260 and following contain an answer to the question posed in what earlier line?

____

12. *ingens* (line 263) modifies what noun? ______________________________

13. Who/what is the understood subject of *geret, contundet,* and *ponet* (lines 263–64)? __________

14. What understood noun is modified by *regnantem* (line 265)? ______________________________

15. *Mavortia* (line 276) is etymologically connected to what noun earlier in the passage? __________

16. What tense are *excipiet, condet,* and *dicet* (lines 276–77)? ______________________________

Essays *Suggested time: 40 minutes (20 minutes per essay)*

1. In line 242, Venus mentions Antenor as someone who has had a fate quite different from that of Aeneas. How does Jupiter's speech further emphasize the different fates of the two men? Present your response in a well-organized essay.

2. It has been argued that Venus is more interested in the future of Rome than she is in the well-being of her son. Based on her speech in lines 229–53, do you agree or disagree? Present your response in a well-organized essay.

For each essay above, support your assertions with references drawn from **throughout** the passage indicated by each essay, i.e., lines 257–77 only for essay #1 and lines 229–53 only for essay #2. All Latin words must be copied or their line numbers provided, AND they must be translated or paraphrased closely enough so that it is clear you understand the Latin. It is your responsibility to convince your reader that you are basing your conclusions on the Latin text and not merely on a general recollection of the passage. Direct your answer to the question; do not merely summarize the passage. Please write your essays on a separate piece of paper.

Scansion

Copy out and scan the line in this passage that contains synizesis.

____

LESSON 7: BOOK I. 278–324

His ego nec metas rerum nec tempora pono:
imperium sine fine dedi. Quin aspera Iuno,
quae mare nunc terrasque metu caelumque fatigat,
consilia in melius referet, mecumque fovebit
Romanos, rerum dominos gentemque togatam.
Sic placitum. Veniet lustris labentibus aetas
cum domus Assaraci Phthiam clarasque Mycenas
servitio premet ac victis dominabitur Argis.
Nascetur pulchra Troianus origine Caesar,
imperium Oceano, famam qui terminet astris,
Iulius, a magno demissum nomen Iulo.
Hunc tu olim caelo spoliis Orientis onustum
accipies secura; vocabitur hic quoque votis.
Aspera tum positis mitescent saecula bellis;
cana Fides, et Vesta, Remo cum fratre Quirinus
iura dabunt; dirae ferro et compagibus artis
claudentur Belli portae; Furor impius intus
saeva sedens super arma et centum vinctus aënis
post tergum nodis fremet horridus ore cruento."
    Haec ait et Maia genitum demittit ab alto,
ut terrae utque novae pateant Karthaginis arces
hospitio Teucris, ne fati nescia Dido
finibus arceret. Volat ille per aëra magnum
remigio alarum ac Libyae citus adstitit oris.
Et iam iussa facit, ponuntque ferocia Poeni
corda volente deo; in primis regina quietum
accipit in Teucros animum mentemque benignam.
    At pius Aeneas per noctem plurima volvens,
ut primum lux alma data est, exire locosque
explorare novos, quas vento accesserit oras,
qui teneant (nam inculta videt), hominesne feraene,
quaerere constituit sociisque exacta referre.
Classem in convexo nemorum sub rupe cavata
arboribus clausam circum atque horrentibus umbris
occulit; ipse uno graditur comitatus Achate
bina manu lato crispans hastilia ferro.
Cui mater media sese tulit obvia silva
virginis os habitumque gerens et virginis arma
Spartanae, vel qualis equos Threissa fatigat
Harpalyce volucremque fuga praevertitur Hebrum.
Namque umeris de more habilem suspenderat arcum
venatrix dederatque comam diffundere ventis,

nuda genu nodoque sinus collecta fluentes.
Ac prior "Heus," inquit, "iuvenes, monstrate mearum
vidistis si quam hic errantem forte sororum
succinctam pharetra et maculosae tegmine lyncis,
aut spumantis apri cursum clamore prementem."

Comprehension Questions

1. What general prophecy does Jupiter make about Roman power? ____________________

2. According to Jupiter, what will Juno feel about the Trojans' descendants? ____________________

3. Where are Phthia and Mycenae, and why does Jupiter mention them here? ____________________

4. What does the use of the epithet *Troianus* in line 286 tell us about *Caesar*? ____________________

5. What type of war does the phrase *Remo cum fratre Quirinus* (line 292) signify? ____________________

6. Why does Jupiter send Mercury to earth? ____________________

7. With what purpose does Aeneas set out? What precaution does he take? ____________________

8. How is Venus dressed? Why, do you think, does Vergil describe her in this way?

9. About whom does Venus ask Aeneas and Achates? ____________________

Short Answer Questions

Indicate True or False.

1. ____ In line 278, *his* refers to Dido and Aeneas.
2. ____ *referet* in line 281 is imperfect subjunctive.
3. ____ Line 282 refers to both the civic and military power of the Romans.
4. ____ Line 288 explains the connection between the Julian *gens* and Aeneas.
5. ____ Another name for *Quirinus* (line 292) is Romulus.
6. ____ In line 296, *horridus* modifies *Furor* (line 294).
7. ____ The subject of *demittit* (line 297) is Mercury.
8. ____ In line 299, *ne* introduces a purpose clause.
9. ____ *ille* in line 300 refers to Aeneas.
10. ____ In line 304, *–que* connects *animum* and *mentem.*
11. ____ Line 305 contains an example of chiasmus.
12. ____ In line 307, *accesserit* is subjunctive in a relative clause of purpose.
13. ____ *inculta* (line 308) is neuter, accusative, plural.
14. ____ In line 309, *constituit* has four complementary infinitives dependent upon it.
15. ____ *clausam* (line 311) modifies *circum.*
16. ____ In line 314, *cui* refers to *Achate.*
17. ____ *Harpalyce* (line 317) is the subject of *praevertitur.*
18. ____ *fluentes* in line 320 is genitive.
19. ____ In line 322, *forte* means "strong," "brave."
20. ____ In line 324, *prementem* modifies *quam* (line 322).

Match each of these Latin nouns or pronouns with the English counterpart.

1.	____ *Phthiam* (line 284)	a.	Mercury
2.	____ *Mycenas* (line 284)	b.	Romulus
3.	____ *Iulo* (line 288)	c.	Augustus
4.	____ *hunc* (line 289)	d.	Carthaginians
5.	____ *Quirinus* (line 292)	e.	Venus
6.	____ *Maia genitum* (line 297)	f.	Aeneas
7.	____ *Teucris* (line 299)	g.	home of Achilles
8.	____ *Poeni* (line 302)	h.	Ascanius
9.	____ *ipse* (line 312)	i.	a river
10.	____ *mater* (line 314)	j.	Trojans
11.	____ *Hebrum* (line 317)	k.	home of Agamemnon

Find an example of each of the following and explain how the figure enhances the meaning of the line. Provide line references in parentheses for your Latin choices.

a. personification ____

____

____

b. simile ____

____

____

c. synchysis ____

____

____

d. alliteration ____

____

____

Translation *Suggested time: 10 minutes*

Translate the passage below as literally as possible.

Classem in convexo nemorum sub rupe cavata
arboribus clausam circum atque horrentibus umbris
occulit; ipse uno graditur comitatus Achate
bina manu lato crispans hastilia ferro.

Essay *Suggested time: 20 minutes*

Jupiter finishes his prophecy with lines 291–96 (*aspera . . . cruento*). Keeping in mind when Vergil was writing the poem, what is the significance of these lines? Present your response in a well-organized essay.

Support your assertions with references drawn from **throughout** this passage (lines 291–96 only). All Latin words must be copied or their line numbers provided, AND they must be translated or paraphrased closely enough so that it is clear you understand the Latin. It is your responsibility to convince your reader that you are basing your conclusions on the Latin text and not merely on a general recollection of the passage. Direct your answer to the question; do not merely summarize the passage. Please write your essay on a separate piece of paper.

Scansion

Scan the following lines.

classem in convexo nemorum sub rupe cavata

arboribus clausam circum atque horrentibus umbris

occulit; ipse uno graditur comitatus Achate

bina manu lato crispans hastilia ferro.

(lines 310–13)

LESSON 8: BOOK I. 325–386

Sic Venus et Veneris contra sic filius orsus:
"Nulla tuarum audita mihi neque visa sororum,
o quam te memorem, virgo? Namque haud tibi vultus
mortalis, nec vox hominem sonat; o, dea certe
(An Phoebi soror? An Nympharum sanguinis una?),
sis felix nostrumque leves, quaecumque, laborem
et quo sub caelo tandem, quibus orbis in oris
iactemur doceas: ignari hominumque locorumque
erramus vento huc vastis et fluctibus acti:
multa tibi ante aras nostra cadet hostia dextra."
Tum Venus: "Haud equidem tali me dignor honore;
virginibus Tyriis mos est gestare pharetram
purpureoque alte suras vincire coturno.
Punica regna vides, Tyrios et Agenoris urbem;
sed fines Libyci, genus intractabile bello.
Imperium Dido Tyria regit urbe profecta,
germanum fugiens. Longa est iniuria, longae
ambages; sed summa sequar fastigia rerum.
Huic coniunx Sychaeus erat, ditissimus auri
Phoenicum, et magno miserae dilectus amore,
cui pater intactam dederat primisque iugarat
ominibus. Sed regna Tyri germanus habebat
Pygmalion, scelere ante alios immanior omnes.
Quos inter medius venit furor. Ille Sychaeum
impius ante aras atque auri caecus amore
clam ferro incautum superat, securus amorum
germanae; factumque diu celavit et aegram
multa malus simulans vana spe lusit amantem.
Ipsa sed in somnis inhumati venit imago
coniugis ora modis attollens pallida miris;
crudeles aras traiectaque pectora ferro
nudavit, caecumque domus scelus omne retexit.
Tum celerare fugam patriaque excedere suadet
auxiliumque viae veteres tellure recludit
thesauros, ignotum argenti pondus et auri.
His commota fugam Dido sociosque parabat.
Conveniunt quibus aut odium crudele tyranni
aut metus acer erat; naves, quae forte paratae,
corripiunt onerantque auro. Portantur avari
Pygmalionis opes pelago; dux femina facti.

Devenere locos ubi nunc ingentia cernes
moenia surgentemque novae Karthaginis arcem,
mercatique solum, facti de nomine Byrsam,
taurino quantum possent circumdare tergo.
Sed vos qui tandem? Quibus aut venistis ab oris?
Quove tenetis iter?" Quaerenti talibus ille
suspirans imoque trahens a pectore vocem:
"O dea, si prima repetens ab origine pergam
et vacet annales nostrorum audire laborum,
ante diem clauso componet Vesper Olympo.
Nos Troia antiqua, si vestras forte per aures
Troiae nomen iit, diversa per aequora vectos
forte sua Libycis tempestas appulit oris.
Sum pius Aeneas, raptos qui ex hoste penates
classe veho mecum, fama super aethera notus;
Italiam quaero patriam, et genus ab Iove summo.
Bis denis Phrygium conscendi navibus aequor,
matre dea monstrante viam data fata secutus;
vix septem convulsae undis Euroque supersunt.
Ipse ignotus, egens, Libyae deserta peragro,
Europa atque Asia pulsus." Nec plura querentem
passa Venus medio sic interfata dolore est:

Comprehension Questions

1. What tone does Aeneas use in greeting his mother in lines 326–29? ____________________

2. Why would Aeneas think that Venus is *Phoebi soror*? ____________________

3. What do you think Aeneas' emotions are as he is speaking in lines 330–34? ____________________

4. Why did Pygmalion kill Sychaeus? ____________________

5. How many times in her speech does Venus use some form of the word *amo* or *amor?* Where in the line does each occur? How many times does she use some form of the word *aurum?*

____

____

6. How does Vergil contrast Dido's love with Pygmalion's? ____________________

____

____

7. Aeneas, who has endured many hardships at this point, chooses only a few to tell to Venus. What does he emphasize? What does this say about his character or what he is feeling?

____

____

____

____

8. Why does Vergil give Venus a speech so much longer than Aeneas'?____________________

____

Multiple Choice Questions *Suggested time: 32 minutes*

1. In Line 329, Aeneas believes Venus may be
   a. Minerva
   b. Phoebe
   c. Juno
   d. Diana

2. The translation of *quaecumque* in line 330 is
   a. whenever
   b. wherever
   c. whatever
   d. whoever

3. In line 332, *ignari* is describing
   a. the Libyans
   b. Aeneas and his men
   c. the waves
   d. the local people

4. In line 332, *iactemur* is
   a. indicative in a direct question
   b. subjunctive in a relative clause of characteristic
   c. indicative in a relative clause
   d. subjunctive in an indirect question

5. The meaning of *hostia* in line 334 is
   a. enemy
   b. stranger
   c. sacrifical victim
   d. host

6. In line 334, *multa* is
   a. ablative singular feminine
   b. accusative plural neuter
   c. nominative singular feminine
   d. nominative plural neuter

7. Line 335 (*haud . . . honore*) is best translated
   a. Indeed not at all do I deem myself worthy of such an honor
   b. Hardly do I deem myself of a certain honor
   c. I am deemed worthy of no such certain honor
   d. Indeed I am not at all deemed worthy by such an honor

8. Venus, in lines 335–37,
   a. explains that all goddesses dress as she does
   b. does not want Aeneas to know that she is his mother
   c. wants to reassure Aeneas that she is not hostile
   d. says that she is hunting in order to gain honor

9. Agenor (line 338) established
   a. Carthage
   b. Troy
   c. Tyre
   d. Libya

10. In line 343, *huic* refers to
    a. Sychaeus (line 343)
    b. Dido (line 340)
    c. Pygmalion (line 347)
    d. pater (line 345)

11. The word that *miserae* (line 344) modifies is
    a. *cui* (line 345)
    b. Dido (understood)
    c. *auri* (line 343)
    d. Sychaeus (line 343)

12. Line 346 contains an example of
    a. polysyndeton
    b. synchysis
    c. chiasmus
    b. metonymy

13. Line 348 contains an example of
    a. zeugma
    b. anastrophe
    c. litotes
    d. anaphora

14. The first four feet of line 349 are scanned
    a. spondee-dactyl-dactyl-spondee
    b. dactyl-spondee-spondee-spondee
    c. spondee-spondee-dactyl-dactyl
    d. dactyl-dactyl-spondee-spondee

15. The understood subject of *celavit* (line 351) and *lusit* (line 352) is
    a. Agenor
    b. Dido
    c. Sychaeus
    d. Pygmalion

16. Lines 353–54 (*ipsa . . . miris*) are best translated
    a. but in a dream came her unburied husband's very image, lifting its pale face in wondrous ways
    b. but her unburied husband came as an image itself in a dream, lifting his face pale in wondrous ways
    c. but the image of her unburied husband came in a dream to her herself lifting her face, pale at the wondrous ways
    d. but in a dream the image of her unburied husband himself came, raising her face pale because of the wondrous ways

17. In line 356, *domus* is
    a. nominative singular
    b. accusative plural
    c. genitive singular
    d. nominative plural

18. In line 357, *–que* connects
    a. *patria* and *excedere*
    b. *celerare* and *excedere*
    c. *fugam* and *patria*
    d. *celerare* and *suadet*

19. To whom does *dux* in line 364 refer?
    a. Dido
    b. Aeneas
    c. Venus
    d. Pygmalion

20. The legend referred to in lines 367–68 arose from the confusion between the Greek word *Byrsam* (line 367) and the Punic word meaning
    a. bull
    b. earth
    c. citadel
    d. wealth

21. In line 370, *quo* is best translated
    a. by what
    b. where/whither
    c. how
    d. why

22. Lines 370–71 (*quaerenti . . . vocem*) are best translated
    a. with her asking such things, he, sighing and drawing his voice from deep in his heart, [replied]
    b. to her asking he, sighing with such [cares] and deeply drawing his voice from his heart, [replied]
    c. to her asking such things, he [replied], sighing deeply and drawing his voice from his heart
    d. to her asking, he, sighing and drawing his voice from deep in his heart, [replied] with such words

23. In line 372, *pergam* is
    a. future indicative
    b. present subjunctive
    c. accusative singular
    d. nominative singular

24. In line 374, *Vesper* refers to
    a. dawn
    b. evening
    c. midnight
    d. noon

25. Aeneas' reference to *raptos penates* (378) shows that
    a. the enemy seized Troy's religious statues
    b. the gods favor Aeneas
    c. he is carrying on Troy's religious practices
    d. he is famous because of Troy's religious statues

26. In line 381, *Phrygium aequor* is located
    a. near Troy
    b. near Carthage
    c. near Italy
    d. near Sicily

Translation *Suggested time: 10 minutes*

Translate the passage below as literally as possible.

Ipsa sed in somnis inhumati venit imago
coniugis ora modis attollens pallida miris;
crudeles aras traiectaque pectora ferro
nudavit, caecumque domus scelus omne retexit.

____

____

____

____

____

Short Answer Questions

From lines 325–34, find, copy out, and provide line references for:

1. a deliberative subjunctive ______
2. and translate three volitive/optative subjunctives ______
3. and scan a line with two elisions ______
4. an adverb formed from a first/second declension adjective ______
5. a nominative plural participle ______

From lines 335–52, find, copy out, and provide line references for:

6. a present participle in the accusative ______
7. two pluperfect verbs ______
8. a clause/sentence with the subject modified by three adjectives ______
9. an objective genitive ______
10. an adverb formed from a first/second declension adjective ______
11. an example of one noun in apposition to another ______

From lines 353–71, find, copy out, and provide line references for:

12. a line that begins with four spondees ______
13. a present participle in the dative ______
14. a third person plural perfect active indicative verb ______
15. a present passive verb ______
16. three present participles in the nominative ______
17. a noun in apposition to another ______
18. an interrogative adjective ______

From lines 372–86, find, copy out, and provide line references for:

19. an example of hyperbole ____________________
20. a phrase that means "twenty" ____________________
21. two present subjunctives in the protasis of a condition ____________________

    ____
22. an adverb that also appears in line 362 ____________________
23. an ablative absolute ____________________
24. a line with two elisions ____________________

Essay *Suggested time: 20 minutes*

Through her narrative of events (lines 338–68), Venus gives a character sketch of Dido. What characteristics of Dido do we see? What sort of person is Dido? How can we tell? Present your response in a well-organized essay.

Support your assertions with references drawn from **throughout** this passage (lines 338–68 only). All Latin words must be copied or their line numbers provided, AND they must be translated or paraphrased closely enough so that it is clear you understand the Latin. It is your responsibility to convince your reader that you are basing your conclusions on the Latin text and not merely on a general recollection of the passage. Direct your answer to the question; do not merely summarize the passage. Please write your essay on a separate piece of paper.

Scansion

Scan the following lines.

Sum pius Aeneas, raptos qui ex hoste penates

classe veho mecum, fama super aethera notus;

Italiam quaero patriam, et genus ab Iove summo.

(lines 378–380)

LESSON 9: BOOK I. 387–440

"Quisquis es, haud, credo, invisus caelestibus auras
vitales carpis, Tyriam qui adveneris urbem;
perge modo atque hinc te reginae ad limina perfer.
Namque tibi reduces socios classemque relatam
nuntio et in tutum versis Aquilonibus actam,
ni frustra augurium vani docuere parentes.
Aspice bis senos laetantes agmine cycnos,
aetheria quos lapsa plaga Iovis ales aperto
turbabat caelo; nunc terras ordine longo
aut capere aut captas iam despectare videntur:
ut reduces illi ludunt stridentibus alis
et coetu cinxere polum cantusque dedere,
haud aliter puppesque tuae pubesque tuorum
aut portum tenet aut pleno subit ostia velo.
Perge modo et, qua te ducit via, dirige gressum."
Dixit et avertens rosea cervice refulsit,
ambrosiaeque comae divinum vertice odorem
spiravere; pedes vestis defluxit ad imos,
et vera incessu patuit dea. Ille ubi matrem
adgnovit tali fugientem est voce secutus:
"Quid natum totiens, crudelis tu quoque, falsis
ludis imaginibus? Cur dextrae iungere dextram
non datur ac veras audire et reddere voces?"
Talibus incusat gressumque ad moenia tendit.
At Venus obscuro gradientes aëre saepsit,
et multo nebulae circum dea fudit amictu,
cernere ne quis eos, neu quis contingere posset
molirive moram aut veniendi poscere causas.
Ipsa Paphum sublimis abit sedesque revisit
laeta suas, ubi templum illi, centumque Sabaeo
ture calent arae sertisque recentibus halant.
Corripuere viam interea, qua semita monstrat.
Iamque ascendebant collem, qui plurimus urbi
imminet adversasque adspectat desuper arces.
Miratur molem Aeneas, magalia quondam,
miratur portas strepitumque et strata viarum.
Instant ardentes Tyrii: pars ducere muros
molirique arcem et manibus subvolvere saxa,
pars optare locum tecto et concludere sulco;
iura magistratusque legunt sanctumque senatum.
Hic portus alii effodiunt; hic alta theatris
fundamenta locant alii, immanesque columnas

rupibus excidunt, scaenis decora alta futuris.
Qualis apes aestate nova per florea rura
exercet sub sole labor, cum gentis adultos
educunt fetus, aut cum liquentia mella
stipant et dulci distendunt nectare cellas,
aut onera accipiunt venientum, aut agmine facto
ignavum fucos pecus a praesepibus arcent;
fervet opus redolentque thymo fraglantia mella.
"O fortunati, quorum iam moenia surgunt!"
Aeneas ait et fastigia suspicit urbis.
Infert se saeptus nebula (mirabile dictu)
per medios, miscetque viris neque cernitur ulli.

Comprehension Questions

1. What about Venus' statement at lines 387–88 is ironic or even untrue? ____________________

____

____

2. In Venus' interpretation of the birds, what does the *Iovis ales* (line 394) represent? What do the *bis senos cycnos* (line 393) represent? How does she conclude from this that some of Aeneas' comrades are safe? ____

____

____

____

3. Why does Venus enclose Aeneas and Achates in a cloud in lines 411–12? ____________________

____

4. What is the effect of the anaphora in lines 421–22? ____________________________________

____

5. In lines 418–29, what phrases show that the various aspects of city life are all being established in Carthage? (Make sure you translate and provide the line references for the phrases that you use to answer the question.)

____

____

____

____

6. What events in the narrative are enhanced by the extended simile (lines 430–36)? ____________

____

____

____

7. What is Aeneas' reaction when he first sees Carthage? ______________________________

____

Multiple Choice Questions *Suggested time: 23 minutes*

1. The meaning of *invisus* (line 387) is
   a. unseen
   b. envied
   c. unexpected
   d. hateful

2. In line 387, *quisquis* is
   a. Venus
   b. Aeneas
   c. Dido
   d. Achates

3. The term *Aquilonibus* (line 391) refers to
   a. a hostile people
   b. strong currents
   c. a sea near Tyria
   d. winds

4. In her augury (lines 393–400), Venus says that
   a. the eagle belongs to Jupiter
   b. six of Aeneas' ships are safe
   c. the Carthaginians are prepared to harm Aeneas and his men
   d. swans are fiercer than they appear

5. The translation of *ut* (line 397) is
   a. as
   b. in order to
   c. with the result that
   d. how

6. Line 399 contains the device
   a. chiasmus
   b. hyperbole
   c. litotes
   d. anaphora

7. In line 407, *quid* is translated
   a. how
   b. what
   c. why
   d. when

8. We know from lines 407–9 that Aeneas feels
   a. betrayed by his mother
   b. that all images are false
   c. that holding his mother's hand is more important than talking
   d. that he has heard the truth from his mother

9. One of the reasons for Venus' actions in lines 411–12 is that
   a. she is afraid someone will kill Aeneas
   b. she wants Aeneas to be more comfortable
   c. she thinks someone will plead a case to Aeneas
   d. she does not want Aeneas delayed by anyone

10. In line 413, *posset* is subjunctive in
    a. an indirect question
    b. a negative purpose clause
    c. a result clause
    d. a clause of fearing

11. Venus goes to Paphus (line 415) because
    a. she was born there
    b. the gods have gathered there
    c. she is worshipped there
    d. one hundred Sabaeans are in the temple there

12. One urban feature Vergil does NOT mention the Carthaginians building (lines 421–29) is
    a. temples
    b. theaters
    c. roads
    d. harbors

13. In line 429, *decora* is in apposition to
    a. *scaenis* (line 429)
    b. *alta* (line 429)
    c. *rupibus* (line 429)
    d. *columnas* (line 428)

14. The subject of *exercet* (line 431) is
    a. *apes* (line 430)
    b. *labor* (line 431)
    c. *rura* (line 430)
    d. *qualis* (line 430)

15. In line 432, *fetus* is
    a. genitive singular
    b. nominative plural
    c. accusative plural
    d. nominative singular

16. Lines 431–32 (*cum . . . fetus*) are best translated
    a. when they lead out the adult offspring of the tribe
    b. when the adults of the tribe lead out the offspring
    c. when the offspring lead out the adult tribes
    d. the offspring lead out the adults with the tribes

17. The first four feet of line 434 are scanned
    a. spondee-spondee-dactyl-dactyl
    b. dactyl-spondee-dactyl-spondee
    c. dactyl-dactyl-dactyl-dactyl
    d. dactyl-dactyl-dactyl-spondee

18. In line 439, *dictu* is translated
    a. by saying
    b. to say
    c. with a word
    d. than a word

19. In line 440, *ulli* is
    a. genitive singular
    b. nominative plural
    c. ablative singular
    d. dative singular

Translation *Suggested time: 10 minutes*

Translate the passage below as literally as possible.

"Quid natum totiens, crudelis tu quoque, falsis
ludis imaginibus? Cur dextrae iungere dextram
non datur ac veras audire et reddere voces?"
Talibus incusat gressumque ad moenia tendit.

____

____

____

____

____

Short Answer Questions

Matching

1.	____ neuter adjective	a.	*adveneris* (line 388)
2.	____ future perfect indicative	b.	*cernere* (line 413)
3.	____ imperfect subjunctive	c.	*dedere* (line 398)
4.	____ complementary infinitive	d.	*frustra* (line 392)
5.	____ superlative adjective	e.	*illi* (line 416)
6.	____ present participle	f.	*incessu* (line 405)
7.	____ gerund	g.	*lapsa* (line 394)
8.	____ perfect participle	h.	*alta* (line 429)
9.	____ ablative of means	i.	*perfer* (line 389)
10.	____ historical infinitive	j.	*plurimus* (line 419)
11.	____ imperative	k.	*posset* (line 413)
12.	____ dative of possession	l.	*subvolvere* (line 424)
13.	____ adverb	m.	*ulli* (line 440)
14.	____ dative of agent	n.	*veniendi* (line 414)
15.	____ perfect indicative	o.	*venientum* (line 434)

Essay *Suggested time: 20 minutes*

Aeneas' cry of despair in lines 407–9 is one of the most poignant in the poem. How does Vergil achieve this effect? Why does Aeneas call his mother *crudelis?* What had he been hoping for that he did not receive from her? Present your response in a well-organized essay.

All Latin words must be copied or their line numbers provided, AND they must be translated or paraphrased closely enough so that it is clear you understand the Latin. It is your responsibility to convince your reader that you are basing your conclusions on the Latin text and not merely on a general recollection of the passage. Direct your answer to the question; do not merely summarize the passage. Please write your essay on a separate piece of paper.

Scansion

Scan the following lines.

instant ardentes Tyrii: pars ducere muros
molirique arcem et manibus subvolvere saxa,
pars optare locum tecto et concludere sulco;

(lines 423–25)

Notes

LESSON 10: BOOK I. 441–493

Lucus in urbe fuit media, laetissimus umbrae,
quo primum iactati undis et turbine Poeni
effodere loco signum, quod regia Iuno
monstrarat, caput acris equi; sic nam fore bello
egregiam et facilem victu per saecula gentem.
Hic templum Iunoni ingens Sidonia Dido
condebat, donis opulentum et numine divae,
aerea cui gradibus surgebant limina nexaeque
aere trabes, foribus cardo stridebat aënis.
Hoc primum in luco nova res oblata timorem
leniit, hic primum Aeneas sperare salutem
ausus et adflictis melius confidere rebus.
Namque sub ingenti lustrat dum singula templo
reginam opperiens, dum quae fortuna sit urbi
artificumque manus inter se operumque laborem
miratur, videt Iliacas ex ordine pugnas
bellaque iam fama totum vulgata per orbem,
Atridas Priamumque et saevum ambobus Achillem.
Constitit et lacrimans "Quis iam locus," inquit, "Achate,
quae regio in terris nostri non plena laboris?
En Priamus. Sunt hic etiam sua praemia laudi,
sunt lacrimae rerum et mentem mortalia tangunt.
Solve metus; feret haec aliquam tibi fama salutem."
Sic ait atque animum pictura pascit inani
multa gemens, largoque umectat flumine vultum.
Namque videbat uti bellantes Pergama circum
hac fugerent Grai, premeret Troiana iuventus;
hac Phryges, instaret curru cristatus Achilles.
Nec procul hinc Rhesi niveis tentoria velis
agnoscit lacrimans, primo quae prodita somno
Tydides multa vastabat caede cruentus,
ardentesque avertit equos in castra prius quam
pabula gustassent Troiae Xanthumque bibissent.
Parte alia fugiens amissis Troilus armis,
infelix puer atque impar congressus Achilli,
fertur equis curruque haeret resupinus inani,
lora tenens tamen; huic cervixque comaeque trahuntur
per terram, et versa pulvis inscribitur hasta.
Interea ad templum non aequae Palladis ibant
crinibus Iliades passis peplumque ferebant
suppliciter, tristes et tunsae pectora palmis;
diva solo fixos oculos aversa tenebat.

Ter circum Iliacos raptaverat Hectora muros
exanimumque auro corpus vendebat Achilles.
Tum vero ingentem gemitum dat pectore ab imo,
ut spolia, ut currus, utque ipsum corpus amici
tendentemque manus Priamum conspexit inermes.
Se quoque principibus permixtum agnovit Achivis,
Eoasque acies et nigri Memnonis arma.
Ducit Amazonidum lunatis agmina peltis
Penthesilea furens mediisque in milibus ardet,
aurea subnectens exsertae cingula mammae
bellatrix, audetque viris concurrere virgo.

Comprehension Questions

1. In lines 441–45, Vergil explains where Juno's temple is located. Why is it located where it is?

    ____

2. How does Vergil show the prosperity of the temple in lines 446–49? ______________________________

    ____

3. How does Aeneas' reaction in lines 450–65 suggest the powerful effect that art can have?

    ____

    ____

    ____

    ____

    ____

4. Aeneas sees seven different scenes depicted on the temple walls (466–93), two described only briefly and five described at greater length. What is depicted in each of these scenes?

    ____

    ____

    ____

    ____

    ____

    ____

    ____

Multiple Choice Questions *Suggested time: 18 minutes*

1. In line 444, *caput* is in apposition to
   a. *quod* (line 443)
   b. *equi* (line 444)
   c. *signum* (line 443)
   d. *Iuno* (line 443)

2. In line 444, *fore* is
   a. ablative
   b. infinitive
   c. subjunctive
   d. accusative

3. In line 452, *et* connects
   a. *sperare* and *confidere*
   b. *ausus* and *adflictis*
   c. *Aeneas* and *melius*
   d. *ausus* and *melius*

4. The form of *melius* in line 452 is
   a. comparative adjective
   b. comparative adverb
   c. positive adjective
   d. positive adverb

5. The case and number of *operum* in line 455 is
   a. accusative singular
   b. nominative singular
   c. accusative plural
   d. genitive plural

6. In line 463, *feret* is
   a. imperfect subjunctive
   b. future indicative
   c. present subjunctive
   d. present indicative

7. The subjunctive verb *premeret* in line 467 is in a(n)
   a. indirect command
   b. result clause
   c. indirect question
   d. purpose clause

8. In line 470, *lacrimans* describes
   a. Aeneas
   b. Rhesus
   c. Achilles
   d. Tydides

9. Line 471 contains
   a. litotes
   b. assonance
   c. hyperbole
   d. chiasmus

10. In line 475, *impar* modifies
    a. Achilles (line 475)
    b. Troilus (line 474)
    c. congressus (line 475)
    d. puer (line 475)

11. Lines 480–81 depict the women of Troy as
    a. mourning
    b. angry
    c. unfair
    d. defeated

12. In line 482, *solo* is translated
    a. by the sun
    b. alone
    c. with one
    d. on the ground

13. The word *corpus* (line 484) refers to
    a. Achilles
    b. Priam
    c. Hector
    d. Troilus

14. In line 486, *ut* is best translated
    a. how
    b. as
    c. in order to
    d. with the result that

15. In line 488, *se* refers to
    a. Priam
    b. Achivis
    c. Aeneas
    d. Eoas

Translation *Suggested time: 10 minutes*

Translate the following passage as literally as possible.

Constitit et lacrimans "quis iam locus," inquit, "Achate,
quae regio in terris nostri non plena laboris?
En Priamus. sunt hic etiam sua praemia laudi,
sunt lacrimae rerum et mentem mortalia tangunt.
Solve metus; feret haec aliquam tibi fama salutem."

Translation and Analysis Questions

Translate the Latin used in the following questions and then answer the question. Also translate the Latin you use in your answers.

From lines 441–45:

1. How does the phrase *egregiam et facilem victu* (line 445) establish the Carthaginians as a worthy opponent of the Romans? ____________________

From lines 446–65:

2. The temple is described as *donis opulentum* (line 447). What other phrases show that the temple is richly decorated? ____________________

3. What exactly is the *nova res* (line 450) which helps to relieve Aeneas' anxiety? ____________________

4. What effect does the fact that the Trojan war is *fama vulgata* (line 457) have? ____________________

5. Why is Achilles described as *saevum ambobus* (line 458)? ____________________

6. Why does Vergil use the adjective *inani* (line 464) to describe the temple pictures? ____________________

From lines 466–93:

7. What does the description of Tydides as *multa caede cruentus* (line 471) make the reader think of him?

8. How does Vergil's identification of Troilus as *infelix puer* (line 475) make Achilles seem even more deadly?

9. Vergil uses the phrase *solo fixos oculos aversa tenebat* (line 482) to describe how Minerva is depicted on the temple. Why is she thus described? What is her reaction to the *Iliades?*

10. Why exactly does Vergil use the phrase *ingentem gemitum* (line 485) to describe Aeneas' response to the ecphrasis?

11. With the words *audetque viris concurrere virgo* (line 494) Vergil draws attention to Penthesilea. What is unusual about her presence here?

Short Answer Questions

Matching

1. ____ *Atridas* (line 458)
2. ____ *Priamum* (line 458)
3. ____ *Achillem* (line 458)
4. ____ *Rhesi* (line 469)
5. ____ *Tydides* (line 471)
6. ____ *Troilus* (line 474)
7. ____ *Palladis* (line 479)
8. ____ *Iliades* (line 480)
9. ____ *Hectora* (line 483)
10. ____ *Memnonis* (line 489)
11. ____ *Penthesilea* (line 491)

a. ally of the Trojans, killed his first night at Troy
b. Amazon ally of the Trojans, killed by Achilles
c. Greek hero, central figure in Homer's *Iliad*
d. Diomedes, a Greek hero
e. Ethiopian ally of the Trojans, killed by Achilles
f. king of Troy who lost sons in the war
g. Minerva
h. son of Priam, killed by Achilles
i. son of Priam, killed and dragged around Troy by Achilles
j. Trojan women
k. the brothers Agamemnon and Menelaus, leaders of the Greeks

Essays *Suggested time: 40 minutes (20 minutes per essay)*

1. One of the ideas Vergil explores in the *Aeneid* is how war affects parents and children. How do the pictures he describes on the temple contribute to this theme? Present your response in a well-organized essay.

2. How is Achilles characterized in this ecphrasis? Why and how does Vergil focus on him here? Present your response in a well-organized essay.

For each essay above, support your assertions with references drawn from the passage. All Latin words must be copied or their line numbers provided, AND they must be translated or paraphrased closely enough so that it is clear you understand the Latin. It is your responsibility to convince your reader that you are basing your conclusions on the Latin text and not merely on a general recollection of the passage. Direct your answer to the question; do not merely summarize the passage. Please write your essays on a separate piece of paper.

Scansion

Scan the following lines.

sic ait atque animum pictura pascit inani

multa gemens, largoque umectat flumine vultum

(lines 464–65)

infelix puer atque impar congressus Achilli

fertur equis curruque haeret resupinus inani

(lines 475–76)

LESSON 11: BOOK I. 494–519

Haec dum Dardanio Aeneae miranda videntur,
dum stupet obtutuque haeret defixus in uno,
regina ad templum, forma pulcherrima Dido,
incessit magna iuvenum stipante caterva.
Qualis in Eurotae ripis aut per iuga Cynthi
exercet Diana choros, quam mille secutae
hinc atque hinc glomerantur Oreades; illa pharetram
fert umero gradiensque deas supereminet omnes
(Latonae tacitum pertemptant gaudia pectus):
talis erat Dido, talem se laeta ferebat
per medios instans operi regnisque futuris.
Tum foribus divae, media testudine templi,
saepta armis solioque alte subnixa resedit.
Iura dabat legesque viris, operumque laborem
partibus aequabat iustis aut sorte trahebat:
cum subito Aeneas concursu accedere magno
Anthea Sergestumque videt fortemque Cloanthum
Teucrorumque alios, ater quos aequore turbo
dispulerat penitusque alias avexerat oras.
Obstipuit simul ipse, simul percussus Achates
laetitiaque metuque; avidi coniungere dextras
ardebant, sed res animos incognita turbat.
Dissimulant et nube cava speculantur amicti
quae fortuna viris, classem quo litore linquant,
quid veniant; cunctis nam lecti navibus ibant
orantes veniam et templum clamore petebant.

Comprehension Questions

1. What is Aeneas doing when Dido enters the temple? ______________________________

____

2. In the simile (lines 498–502), to whom or what is the *magna iuvenum stipante caterva* compared?

____

3. Why is Leto happy? ____

4. Why does Vergil depict Dido performing the acts she does in lines 507–8? ______

5. What is *the res incognita* of line 515? ______

6. What are Aeneas' comrades doing? ______

Short Answer Questions

1. How is *dum* (lines 494 and 495) translated? ______
2. What case is *Aeneae* (line 494)? ______
3. What case is *forma* (line 496)? ______
4. How is the phrase *magna iuvenum stipante caterva* (line 497) translated? ______
5. What poetic device does *qualis* (line 498) introduce? ______
6. What is the antecedent of *quam* (line 499)? ______
7. What does *secutae* (line 499) modify? ______
8. Who/what is *illa* (line 500)? ______
9. What is the subject of *pertemptant* (line 502)? ______
10. Who/what does *saepta* (line 506) describe? ______
11. Who/what is the subject of *aequabat* (line 508)? ______
12. Why is *accedere* (line 509) in the infinitive? ______
13. Who/what is the antecedent of *quos* (line 511)? ______
14. Who is *ipse* (line 513)? ______
15. Who/what does *avidi* (line 514) describe? ______
16. Why are *linquant* (line 517) and *veniant* (line 518) in the subjunctive? ______
17. Who/what does *lecti* (line 518) describe? ______

Translation *Suggested time: 15 minutes*

Translate the following passage as literally as possible.

Iura dabat legesque viris, operumque laborem
partibus aequabat iustis aut sorte trahebat:
cum subito Aeneas concursu accedere magno
Anthea Sergestumque videt fortemque Cloanthum
Teucrorumque alios, ater quos aequore turbo
dispulerat penitusque alias avexerat oras.

____

____

____

____

____

____

____

Essays *Suggested time: 40 minutes (20 minutes per essay)*

1. By comparing Dido to Diana (lines 498–504), what does Vergil suggest about Dido? Present your response in a well-organized essay.

2. What is Aeneas feeling in lines 513–19? Present your response in a well-organized essay.

For each essay above, support your assertions with references drawn from **throughout** the passage indicated by each essay, i.e., lines 498–504 for essay #1 and lines 513–519 for essay #2. All Latin words must be copied or their line numbers provided, AND they must be translated or paraphrased closely enough so that it is clear you understand the Latin. It is your responsibility to convince your reader that you are basing your conclusions on the Latin text and not merely on a general recollection of the passage. Direct your answer to the question; do not merely summarize the passage. Please write your essays on a separate piece of paper.

Scansion

Scan the following lines.

dum stupet obtutuque haeret defixus in uno,

regina ad templum, forma pulcherrima Dido,

(lines 495–96)

saepta armis solioque alte subnixa resedit. (line 506)

Book I Comprehensive Review Essay

Using your knowledge of the gods as depicted in Book 1, discuss the nature of divine-human relations in the *Aeneid*. In your answer, refer to the depictions of at least three different gods who appear in Book 1. Please write your essay on a separate piece of paper.

THE *AENEID*
BOOK II SELECTIONS WITH EXERCISES

LESSON 12: BOOK II. 1–56

Conticuere omnes intentique ora tenebant;
inde toro pater Aeneas sic orsus ab alto:
"Infandum, regina, iubes renovare dolorem,
Troianas ut opes et lamentabile regnum
eruerint Danai, quaeque ipse miserrima vidi
et quorum pars magna fui. Quis talia fando
Myrmidonum Dolopumve aut duri miles Ulixi
temperet a lacrimis? Et iam nox umida caelo
praecipitat suadentque cadentia sidera somnos.
Sed si tantus amor casus cognoscere nostros
et breviter Troiae supremum audire laborem,
quamquam animus meminisse horret luctuque refugit
incipiam. Fracti bello fatisque repulsi
ductores Danaum tot iam labentibus annis
instar montis equum divina Palladis arte
aedificant, sectaque intexunt abiete costas;
votum pro reditu simulant; ea fama vagatur.
Huc delecta virum sortiti corpora furtim
includunt caeco lateri penitusque cavernas
ingentes uterumque armato milite complent.
Est in conspectu Tenedos, notissima fama
insula, dives opum Priami dum regna manebant,
nunc tantum sinus et statio male fida carinis:
huc se provecti deserto in litore condunt;
nos abiisse rati et vento petiisse Mycenas.
Ergo omnis longo solvit se Teucria luctu;
panduntur portae, iuvat ire et Dorica castra
desertosque videre locos litusque relictum:
hic Dolopum manus, hic saevus tendebat Achilles;
classibus hic locus, hic acie certare solebant.
Pars stupet innuptae donum exitiale Minervae
et molem mirantur equi; primusque Thymoetes
duci intra muros hortatur et arce locari,
sive dolo seu iam Troiae sic fata ferebant.
At Capys, et quorum melior sententia menti,
aut pelago Danaum insidias suspectaque dona
praecipitare iubent subiectisque urere flammis,
aut terebrare cavas uteri et temptare latebras.
Scinditur incertum studia in contraria vulgus.
Primus ibi ante omnes magna comitante caterva
Laocoon ardens summa decurrit ab arce,
et procul 'O miseri, quae tanta insania, cives?

Creditis avectos hostis? Aut ulla putatis
dona carere dolis Danaum? Sic notus Ulixes?
Aut hoc inclusi ligno occultantur Achivi,
aut haec in nostros fabricata est machina muros,
inspectura domos venturaque desuper urbi,
aut aliquis latet error; equo ne credite, Teucri.
Quidquid id est, timeo Danaos et dona ferentes.'
Sic fatus validis ingentem viribus hastam
in latus inque feri curvam compagibus alvum
contorsit. Stetit illa tremens, uteroque recusso
insonuere cavae gemitumque dedere cavernae.
Et, si fata deum, si mens non laeva fuisset,
impulerat ferro Argolicas foedare latebras,
Troiaque nunc staret, Priamique arx alta maneres.

Comprehension Questions

1. Why does Aeneas use the phrase *infandum dolorem* (line 3) to describe the subject of his story? What other phrases, with line numbers, does he use that emphasize the same tone?

____

____

____

2. Under what pretext had the Greeks built the horse? ______________________________

____

3. In line 26, what emotion does Aeneas attribute to the Trojans? ______________________________

4. What are the two sides of the debate about the horse? What does each side want to do? ________

____

____

____

5. What case does Laocoon make (lines 42–49) for not accepting the horse into the city? ________

____

____

6. The contrary-to-fact condition in lines 54–56 evokes what emotions? ______________________________

____

____

Multiple Choice Questions *Suggested time: 25 minutes*

1. In line 1, *conticuere* is
   a. imperative
   b. infinitive
   c. indicative
   d. subjunctive

2. In line 4, *ut* is translated
   a. how
   b. as
   c. in order to
   d. with the result that

3. The subject of *eruerint* (line 5) is
   a. *opes* (line 4)
   b. *Danai* (line 5)
   c. *quae* (line 5)
   d. they [understood]

4. In lines 8–9 (*et iam . . . somnos*) we learn that
   a. it is late at night
   b. the Greeks attacked Troy at night
   c. it is raining
   d. the Greeks were weary after the ten-year siege

5. *Troiae* (line 11) is
   a. dative
   b. genitive
   c. nominative
   d. ablative

6. In line 14, *Danaum* is
   a. accusative singular
   b. genitive plural
   c. nominative singular
   d. dative plural

7. In line 15, *Palladis* is mentioned because
   a. he built the horse
   b. the horse is sacred to her
   c. she is the goddess of wisdom and crafts
   d. he conceived the idea of the horse

8. The meaning of *huc* in line 18 is
   a. to this place
   b. from this place
   c. by this place
   d. at this place

9. *Tenedos* (line 21) is near
   a. Mycenae
   b. Sicily
   c. Carthage
   d. Troy

10. In line 22, *dives* is
    a. nominative singular
    b. nominative plural
    c. accusative plural
    d. accusative singular

11. Line 23 contains an example of
    a. anaphora
    b. chiasmus
    c. litotes
    d. metonymy

12. The translation of *rati* (line 25) is
    a. having thought
    b. we thought
    c. they thought
    d. having been thought

13. In lines 29–30 (*hic . . . solebant*)
    a. the Dolopes fight with Achilles and his battle line
    b. Achilles heads toward the Dolopes with his fleet
    c. the Trojans strive to fight with the Dolopes and Achilles
    d. the Trojans look at the sites where the Greeks had been and fought

14. In line 33, the form of *duci* is
    a. genitive
    b. dative
    c. an infinitive
    d. an imperative

15. In line 39, *vulgus* is
    a. nominative singular
    b. genitive singular
    c. accusative singular
    d. accusative plural

16. Line 45 contains an example of
    a. alliteration
    b. metonymy
    c. anastrophe
    d. hyperbaton

17. *Teucri* in line 48 is
    a. genitive
    b. nominative
    c. vocative
    d. ablative

18. In line 52, *illa* refers to
    a. *hastam* (line 50)
    b. *curvam* (line 51)
    c. *cavae* (line 53)
    d. *alvum* (line 51)

19. In line 56, *staret* is translated
    a. was standing
    b. would stand
    c. will stand
    d. might have stood

20. Line 56 contains an example of
    a. anaphora
    b. hyperbole
    c. apostrophe
    d. hendiadys

Translation *Suggested time: 15 minutes*

Translate the following passage as literally as possible.

Sed si tantus amor casus cognoscere nostros
et breviter Troiae supremum audire laborem,
quamquam animus meminisse horret luctuque refugit
incipiam. Fracti bello fatisque repulsi
ductores Danaum tot iam labentibus annis
instar montis equum divina Palladis arte
aedificant, sectaque intexunt abiete costas;

Translation and Analysis Questions

Translate the Latin in each question below and answer the question.

1. Aeneas says, in lines 6–8, *"Quis talia fando/ Myrmidonum Dolopumve aut duri miles Ulixi/ temperet a lacrimis?"* What point is he making?

2. What metaphor is created with the use of the word *uterum* (line 20)?

3. Aeneas explains the Trojans' fatal mistake with the words *nos abiisse rati et vento petiisse Mycenas* (line 25). Why did they believe this?

4. Why does Aeneas use the phrase *melior sententia menti* (line 35) to describe Capys and others?

5. What is the *tanta insania* (line 42) that Laocoon mentions?

Short Answer Questions

Give the direct object(s) of the following:

1. *tenebant* (line 1) __________
2. *vidi* (line 5) __________
3. *fando* (line 6) __________
4. *suadent* (line 9) __________
5. *aedificant* (line 16) __________

6. *includunt* (line 19) ______________________________

7. *condunt* (line 24) ______________________________

8. *solvit* (line 26)______________________________

9. *stupet* (line 31) ______________________________

10. *ferentes* (line 49)______________________________

11. *contorsit* (line 52) ______________________________

12. *dedere* (line 53)______________________________

Essay *Suggested time: 20 minutes*

In this passage (lines 1–56), Vergil foreshadows the doom of Troy. In a well-organized essay, show how Vergil does this.

Support your assertions with references drawn from **throughout** the passage. All Latin words must be copied or their line numbers provided, AND they must be translated or paraphrased closely enough so that it is clear you understand the Latin. It is your responsibility to convince your reader that you are basing your conclusions on the Latin text and not merely on a general recollection of the passage. Direct your answer to the question; do not merely summarize the passage. Please write your essay on a separate piece of paper.

Scansion

Scan the following lines.

aut pelago Danaum insidias suspectaque dona

praecipitare iubent subiectisque urere flammis

aut terebrare cavas uteri et temptare latebras

(lines 36–38)

LESSON 13: BOOK II. 199–249

Hic aliud maius miseris multoque tremendum
obicitur magis atque improvida pectora turbat.
Laocoon, ductus Neptuno sorte sacerdos,
sollemnes taurum ingentem mactabat ad aras.
Ecce autem gemini a Tenedo tranquilla per alta
(horresco referens) immensis orbibus angues
incumbunt pelago pariterque ad litora tendunt;
pectora quorum inter fluctus arrecta iubaeque
sanguineae superant undas, pars cetera pontum
pone legit sinuatque immensa volumine terga.
Fit sonitus spumante salo; iamque arva tenebant
ardentesque oculos suffecti sanguine et igni
sibila lambebant linguis vibrantibus ora.
Diffugimus visu exsangues. Illi agmine certo
Laocoonta petunt; et primum parva duorum
corpora natorum serpens amplexus uterque
implicat et miseros morsu depascitur artus;
post ipsum auxilio subeuntem ac tela ferentem
corripiunt spirisque ligant ingentibus; et iam
bis medium amplexi, bis collo squamea circum
terga dati superant capite et cervicibus altis.
Ille simul manibus tendit divellere nodos
perfusus sanie vittas atroque veneno,
clamores simul horrendos ad sidera tollit:
qualis mugitus, fugit cum saucius aram
taurus et incertam excussit cervice securim.
At gemini lapsu delubra ad summa dracones
effugiunt saevaeque petunt Tritonidis arcem,
sub pedibusque deae clipeique sub orbe teguntur.
Tum vero tremefacta novus per pectora cunctis
insinuat pavor, et scelus expendisse merentem
Laocoonta ferunt, sacrum qui cuspide robur
laeserit et tergo sceleratam intorserit hastam.
Ducendum ad sedes simulacrum orandaque divae
numina conclamant.
Dividimus muros et moenia pandimus urbis.
Accingunt omnes operi pedibusque rotarum
subiciunt lapsus, et stuppea vincula collo
intendunt: scandit fatalis machina muros
feta armis. Pueri circum innuptaeque puellae
sacra canunt funemque manu contingere gaudent;

illa subit mediaeque minans inlabitur urbi.
O patria, o divum domus Ilium et incluta bello
moenia Dardanidum! Quater ipso in limine portae
substitit atque utero sonitum quater arma dedere;
instamus tamen immemores caecique furore
et monstrum infelix sacrata sistimus arce.
Tunc etiam fatis aperit Cassandra futuris
ora dei iussu non umquam credita Teucris.
Nos delubra deum miseri, quibus ultimus esset
ille dies, festa velamus fronde per urbem.

Comprehension Questions

1. What was Laocoon doing when the snakes were coming ashore? ______________________

   ____

2. What two Greek leaders do the two snakes (lines 203–4) symbolize? ______________________

   ____

3. What event in the narrative is enhanced by the simile (lines 223–24)? ______________________

   ____

4. What is the result of Laocoon's death? ______________________

   ____

5. What omen/sign do the Trojans ignore as they drag the horse into the city? ______________________

   ____

6. Copy out and give the line numbers for all the words related to snakes or snake imagery in this passage.

   ____

   ____

   ____

   ____

Multiple Choice Questions *Suggested time: 25 minutes*

1. What part of speech is the word *maius* (line 199)?
   a. noun
   b. adverb
   c. adjective
   d. preposition

2. Lines 201–2 (*Laocoon . . . aras*) tell us that Laocoon
   a. had been led to Neptune's priest
   b. was solemn before the temple of Neptune
   c. had led a bull to Neptune
   d. was sacrificing a bull

3. The case and number of *fluctus* (line 206) is
   a. accusative plural
   b. nominative plural
   c. nominative singular
   d. genitive singular

4. What part of speech is *pone* (line 208)?
   a. noun
   b. verb
   c. adverb
   d. adjective

5. From line 212 (*diffugimus . . . exsangues*), we can infer that
   a. the snakes were bloodless
   b. the Trojans were afraid
   c. most Trojans escaped from the snakes
   d. the snakes were bloody in their sight

6. From lines 213–15 (*et . . . artus*), we can infer that
   a. Laocoon's sons were young
   b. the bodies of the snakes were small
   c. Laocoon loved his sons
   d. Lacoon's sons embraced each other in their fear

7. The words *miseros . . . artus* (line 215) are translated
   a. the limb with respect to the wretched ones is fed upon with a bite
   b. [each] feeds upon the limbs with a wretched bite
   c. the limbs of the wretched ones are fed upon with a bite
   d. [each] feeds upon the wretched limbs with its bite

8. In line 221, *perfusus* describes
   a. *sanie* (line 221)
   b. *nodos* (line 220)
   c. *ille* (line 220)
   d. *vittas* (line 221)

9. Lines 223–24 (*qualis . . . securim*) tell us that
   a. the bull Laocoon was sacrificing fled
   b. Laocoon was screaming like a wounded bull
   c. Laocoon, wounded, fled to the altar
   d. the bull fled with uncertainty because it was wounded

10. Another name for *Tritonidis* (line 226) is
    a. Minerva
    b. Juno
    c. Triton
    d. Neptune

11. Lines 229–30 (*et . . . ferunt*) tell us that
    a. the Trojans carried off Laocoon's body after he died
    b. Laocoon had carefully considered his wrongdoing
    c. the Trojans felt Laocoon deserved his death
    d. the Trojans mourned for Laocoon because of his penalty

12. The tense and mood of *laeserit* (line 231) is
    a. perfect indicative
    b. pluperfect subjunctive
    c. future perfect indicative
    d. perfect subjunctive

13. The metrical pattern of the first four feet of line 232 is
    a. spondee-spondee-dactyl-dactyl
    b. spondee-spondee-dactyl-spondee
    c. dactyl-dactyl-dactyl-spondee
    d. dactyl-dactyl-spondee-dactyl

14. In line 232, *simulacrum* refers to
    a. the spear
    b. the statue of the goddess
    c. the horse
    d. Laocoon

15. The words *scandit . . . armis* (lines 237–38) are translated
    a. the machine climbs the deadly walls, pregnant with arms
    b. the deadly machine, pregnant with weapons, climbs the walls
    c. the machine, pregnant with deadly weapons, climbs the walls
    d. the walls are mounted by the machine pregnant with deadly weapons

16. In line 240, *illa* refers to
    a. *machina* (line 237)
    b. *puellae* (line 238)
    c. *sacra* (line 239)
    d. *urbi* (line 240)

17. What figure of speech occurs in line 241–42 (*o . . . Dardanidum*)?
    a. hendiadys
    b. tmesis
    c. zeugma
    d. apostrophe

18. Line 244 (*instamus . . . furore*) tells us that the Trojans
    a. thought Laocoon was heedless and furious
    b. were not thinking clearly
    c. were furious
    d. pressed on although they remembered Laocoon's madness

19. The word *Teucris* (line 247) is translated
    a. for the Trojans
    b. of the Trojans
    c. by the Trojans
    d. with the Trojans

20. In line 248, *quibus* refers to
    a. *nos* (line 248)
    b. *delubra* (line 248)
    c. *dies* (line 249)
    d. *dei* (line 247)

Translation *Suggested time: 10 minutes*

Translate the following lines as literally as possible.

Ille simul manibus tendit divellere nodos
perfusus sanie vittas atroque veneno,
clamores simul horrendos ad sidera tollit:
qualis mugitus, fugit cum saucius aram
taurus et incertam excussit cervice securim.

Essays *Suggested time: 40 minutes (20 minutes per essay)*

1. The description of the snakes and their actions (lines 203–227) is extraordinarily vivid. How does Vergil achieve this effect? What senses does his description include? Present your response in a well-organized essay.

2. In lines 234–49 Aeneas emphasizes with regret the rashness of the Trojans in bringing the horse into their city. How does he convey this? Present your response in a well-organized essay.

For each essay above, support your assertions with references drawn from **throughout** the passage indicated by each essay, i.e., lines 203–227 only for essay #1 and lines 234–49 for essay #2. All Latin words must be copied or their line numbers provided, AND they must be translated or paraphrased closely enough so that it is clear you understand the Latin. It is your responsibility to convince your reader that you are basing your conclusions on the Latin text and not merely on a general recollection of the passage. Direct your answer to the question; do not merely summarize the passage. Please write your essays on a separate piece of paper.

Scansion

Scan the following lines.

incumbunt pelago pariterque ad litora tendunt;

pectora quorum inter fluctus arrecta iubaeque

sanguineae superant undas, pars cetera pontum

pone legit sinuatque immensa volumine terga.

(lines 205–208)

LESSON 14: BOOK II. 250–97

Vertitur interea caelum et ruit Oceano nox
involvens umbra magna terramque polumque
Myrmidonumque dolos; fusi per moenia Teucri
conticuere; sopor fessos complectitur artus.
Et iam Argiva phalanx instructis navibus ibat
a Tenedo tacitae per amica silentia lunae
litora nota petens, flammas cum regia puppis
extulerat, fatisque deum defensus iniquis
inclusos utero Danaos et pinea furtim
laxat claustra Sinon. Illos patefactus ad auras
reddit equus laetique cavo se robore promunt
Thessandrus Sthenelusque duces et dirus Ulixes,
demissum lapsi per funem, Acamasque Thoasque
Pelidesque Neoptolemus primusque Machaon
et Menelaus et ipse doli fabricator Epeos.
Invadunt urbem somno vinoque sepultam;
caeduntur vigiles, portisque patentibus omnes
accipiunt socios atque agmina conscia iungunt.
Tempus erat quo prima quies mortalibus aegris
incipit et dono divum gratissima serpit.
In somnis, ecce, ante oculos maestissimus Hector
visus adesse mihi largosque effundere fletus,
raptatus bigis ut quondam, aterque cruento
pulvere perque pedes traiectus lora tumentes.
Ei mihi, qualis erat, quantum mutatus ab illo
Hectore qui redit exuvias indutus Achilli
vel Danaum Phrygios iaculatus puppibus ignes;
squalentem barbam et concretos sanguine crines
vulneraque illa gerens, quae circum plurima muros
accepit patrios. Ultro flens ipse videbar
compellare virum et maestas expromere voces:
'O lux Dardaniae, spes o fidissima Teucrum,
quae tantae tenuere morae? Quibus Hector ab oris
exspectate venis? Ut te post multa tuorum
funera, post varios hominumque urbisque labores
defessi aspicimus! Quae causa indigna serenos
foedavit vultus? Aut cur haec vulnera cerno?'
Ille nihil, nec me quaerentem vana moratur,
sed graviter gemitus imo de pectore ducens,
'Heu fuge, nate dea, teque his' ait 'eripe flammis.
Hostis habet muros; ruit alto a culmine Troia.
Sat patriae Priamoque datum: si Pergama dextra

defendi possent, etiam hac defensa fuissent.
Sacra suosque tibi commendat Troia penates;
hos cape fatorum comites, his moenia quaere
magna, pererrato statues quae denique ponto.'
Sic ait et manibus vittas Vestamque potentem
aeternumque adytis effert penetralibus ignem.

Comprehension Questions

1. How does Vergil establish the time for this episode? ______________________________

   ____

2. How is the metaphor of pregnancy and birth continued here from the previous passage?

   ____

3. Vergil here begins to use fire and flame imagery which will continue throughout Book II. Copy out all the words, with their line numbers, that are tied to this image.

   ____

   ____

   ____

4. How does Hector look when he appears to Aeneas? Why does he look this way? __________

   ____

   ____

5. What is Aeneas' reaction when he sees Hector? ______________________________

   ____

6. What instructions does Hector give Aeneas? ______________________________

   ____

7. Hector boasts a bit in lines 291–292. What does he say?

   ____

   ____

   ____

8. What does Hector do in the final two lines of this passage? What do you think the significance of this is? ____

   ____

Short Answer Questions

Indicate True or False.

1. ____ *magna* (line 251) modifies *nox.*
2. ____ The first word of line 253 is also the first word of Book II.
3. ____ *Pelides* (line 263) is a reminder of the wedding where the Trojan war was instigated.
4. ____ *ipse* (line 264) modifies *Epeos.*
5. ____ In line 268 *quo* is translated "by which."
6. ____ *gratissima* (line 269) modifies *quies.*
7. ____ *fletus* in line 271 is nominative singular.
8. ____ *Phrygios* (line 276) refers to the Greeks.
9. ____ In line 279, *ipse* is translated "I myself."
10. ____ *spes* (line 281) refers to Hector.
11. ____ *quae* in line 285 is accusative, plural, neuter.
12. ____ In line 287, *vana* is the object of *quaerentem.*
13. ____ *dea* (line 289) is vocative.
14. ____ *commendat* in line 293 is present subjunctive.
15. ____ *potentem* (line 296) and *aeternum* (line 297) both modify *ignem.*

Translation *Suggested time: 10 minutes*

Translate the following passage as literally as possible.

Sat patriae Priamoque datum: si Pergama dextra
defendi possent, etiam hac defensa fuissent.
Sacra suosque tibi commendat Troia penates;
hos cape fatorum comites, his moenia quaere
magna, pererrato statues quae denique ponto.'

Short Answer Questions

From lines 250–67, find, copy out, and provide line references in parentheses for:

1. a perfect participle of a deponent verb ______
2. an example of hysteron proteron ______
3. a patronymic ______
4. a third person plural perfect active indicative verb ______
5. two ablatives absolute ______
6. an example of zeugma ______
7. three objects of *involvens* (line 251) ______
8. seven perfect participles passive in form and meaning ______
9. a second declension genitive plural in *–um* ______

From lines 268–97, find, copy out, and provide line references in parentheses for:

10. an ablative absolute ______
11. two neuter relative pronouns ______
12. a verb in the future tense ______
13. a passive infinitive ______
14. a perfect passive participle in the vocative ______
15. four superlative adjectives ______
16. three nouns in the vocative ______
17. three objects of *gerens* (line 278) ______
18. a reflexive pronoun in the accusative ______
19. a reflexive adjective in the accusative ______
20. the object of *ducens* (line 288) ______

Translation and Analysis Questions

1. Readers and commentators have long noted that darkness is the context for many disasters and acts of treachery in the *Aeneid.* Find and translate a phrase from lines 250–53 that supports this statement. ____________________

2. The noun *artus* (line 253) also occurred as a direct object in line 215, and *complectitur* (line 253) is related to *amplexus* (line 214) and *amplexi* (line 218). Comparing these lines, what conclusions can you draw about the tone or the nature of the foreshadowing of line 253?

3. Find and translate words and phrases from lines 254–59 (*et . . . Sinon*) that anticipate that the Greeks will be successful. ____________________

4. Vergil delays the list of Greek heroes until after the verb (*promunt,* line 260) and then gives nine Greek names in four lines. What is the effect of this? ____________________

5. Why might Vergil have used the word *sepultam* (line 265)? ____________________

6. Why do you think Vergil used the verb *serpit* (line 269)? ____________________

7. From lines 270–79, copy out and translate the phrases that describe Hector's appearance. How does his appearance affect the reader?

8. What effect do the lines 274–76 have? ____________________

9. What feelings about Hector does Aeneas express in his speech (lines 281–86)? Copy out and translate three phrases to support your answer.

10. How does Hector's statement at line 293 support an aspect of Aeneas' character that Vergil has emphasized earlier in the poem? ____________________

Essay *Suggested time: 20 minutes*

Descriptions of sleep and imagery associated with sleep permeate this passage (lines 250–297). Find in this passage at least five words or phrases associated with sleep. What tone do they set for the appearance of Hector in Aeneas' dream? Present your response in a well-organized essay.

Support your assertions with references drawn from **throughout** the passage (lines 250–297). All Latin words must be copied or their line numbers provided, AND they must be translated or paraphrased closely enough so that it is clear you understand the Latin. It is your responsibility to convince your reader that you are basing your conclusions on the Latin text and not merely on a general recollection of the passage. Direct your answer to the question; do not merely summarize the passage. Please write your essay on a separate piece of paper.

Scansion

Scan the following lines.

Vertitur interea caelum et ruit Oceano nox (line 250)

Et iam Argiva phalanx instructis navibus ibat (line 254)

LESSON 15: BOOK II. 469–525

Vestibulum ante ipsum primoque in limine Pyrrhus
exsultat telis et luce coruscus aëna:
qualis ubi in lucem coluber mala gramina pastus,
frigida sub terra tumidum quem bruma tegebat,
nunc, positis novus exuviis nitidusque iuventa,
lubrica convolvit sublato pectore terga
arduus ad solem, et linguis micat ore trisulcis.
Una ingens Periphas et equorum agitator Achillis,
armiger Automedon, una omnis Scyria pubes
succedunt tecto et flammas ad culmina iactant.
Ipse inter primos correpta dura bipenni
limina perrumpit postesque a cardine vellit
aeratos; iamque excisa trabe firma cavavit
robora et ingentem lato dedit ore fenestram.
apparet domus intus et atria longa patescunt;
apparent Priami et veterum penetralia regum,
armatosque vident stantes in limine primo.
At domus interior gemitu miseroque tumultu
miscetur, penitusque cavae plangoribus aedes
femineis ululant; ferit aurea sidera clamor.
Tum pavidae tectis matres ingentibus errant
amplexaeque tenent postes atque oscula figunt.
Instat vi patria Pyrrhus; nec claustra nec ipsi
custodes sufferre valent; labat ariete crebro
ianua, et emoti procumbunt cardine postes.
Fit via vi; rumpunt aditus primosque trucidant
immissi Danai et late loca milite complent.
Non sic, aggeribus ruptis cum spumeus amnis
exiit oppositasque evicit gurgite moles,
fertur in arva furens cumulo camposque per omnes
cum stabulis armenta trahit. Vidi ipse furentem
caede Neoptolemum geminosque in limine Atridas,
vidi Hecubam centumque nurus Priamumque per aras
sanguine foedantem quos ipse sacraverat ignes.
Quinquaginta illi thalami, spes tanta nepotum,
barbarico postes auro spoliisque superbi
procubuere; tenent Danai qua deficit ignis.
Forsitan et Priami fuerint quae fata requiras.
Urbis uti captae casum convulsaque vidit
limina tectorum et medium in penetralibus hostem,
arma diu senior desueta trementibus aevo
circumdat nequiquam umeris et inutile ferrum

cingitur, ac densos fertur moriturus in hostes.
Aedibus in mediis nudoque sub aetheris axe
ingens ara fuit iuxtaque veterrima laurus
incumbens arae atque umbra complexa penates.
Hic Hecuba et natae nequiquam altaria circum,
praecipites atra ceu tempestate columbae,
condensae et divum amplexae simulacra sedebant.
Ipsum autem sumptis Priamum iuvenalibus armis
ut vidit, 'Quae mens tam dira, miserrime coniunx,
impulit his cingi telis? Aut quo ruis?' inquit.
'Non tali auxilio nec defensoribus istis
tempus eget; non, si ipse meus nunc adforet Hector.
Huc tandem concede; haec ara tuebitur omnes,
aut moriere simul.' Sic ore effata recepit
ad sese et sacra longaevum in sede locavit.

Comprehension Questions

1. How does the simile in lines 471–75 make the description of Pyrrhus especially vivid? What visual aspect of Pyrrhus is emphasized by this simile? ______________________

____

____

2. With the simile (lines 471–75) Vergil continues his use of snake imagery. How does this description of Pyrrhus reinforce the earlier images of snakes in the Laocoon passage? ____________

____

____

3. Although the warrior Achilles is not present in these lines, Vergil reminds the reader of Achilles' existence in at least two ways in lines 469–78. How does Vergil do this? ____________

____

____

4. In lines 483–90, how does Vergil emphasize both the visual and the aural aspects of the scene?

____

____

5. In line 491, what phrase again reminds the reader of Achilles' deadly nature? ______________

____

6. How does the simile at lines 496–99 illuminate the action of the narrative? ______________

____

____

7. What adjective is used to describe *Neoptolemum* (line 500)? This word and its noun counterpart are used frequently in the poem. What does Vergil mean by using these words so frequently?

____

____

8. In lines 499–502, Aeneas names five people and one group whom he saw in the palace. Who are they? ______________________________

____

____

9. In line 503, Vergil emphasizes again, as he did in line 501, the theme of generations and, by implication, how war destroys any expectation of future generations. With what words does he do this?______________________________

____

____

10. Lines 509–11 are especially poignant. How and why does Vergil characterize Priam in the way that he does?______________________________

____

____

____

____

11. How does the simile in line 516 further our understanding of the feelings of Hecuba and her daughters?______________________________

____

____

12. What is the tone of Hecuba's speech in lines 519–24? Find and translate at least one phrase to support your answer.

____

____

____

13. Priam's name occurs four times in this passage. Why is Vergil focusing on him here? __________

____

____

____

____

Multiple Choice Questions *Suggested time: 18 minutes*

1. In line 472, *frigida* modifies
   a. *mala* (line 471)
   b. *gramina* (line 471)
   c. *terra* (line 472)
   d. *bruma* (line 472)

2. The antecedent of *quem* (line 472) is
   a. *coluber* (line 471)
   b. *terra* (line 472)
   c. *tumidum* (line 472)
   d. *bruma* (line 472)

3. The simile in lines 471–75 emphasizes that
   a. snakes are deadly
   b. Pyrrhus' armor is shiny
   c. Pyrrhus is deadly
   d. Pyrrhus is on the threshold

4. Line 474 contains an example of
   a. synchysis
   b. litotes
   c. chiasmus
   d. hyperbole

5. In line 479, *ipse* refers to
   a. Pyrrhus
   b. Achilles
   c. Automedon
   d. Scyria

6. The word *excisa* (line 481) modifies
   a. *cardine* (line 480)
   b. *firma* (line 481)
   c. *trabe* (line 481)
   d. *robora* (line 482)

7. In line 486, *–que* connects
   a. *interior* and *tumultu*
   b. *domus* and *misero*
   c. *misero* and *tumultu*
   d. *gemitu* and *tumultu*

8. Line 488 contains an example of
   a. hyperbole
   b. anaphora
   c. aposiopesis
   d. hendiadys

9. The antecedent of *quos* (line 502) is
   a. *aras* (line 501)
   b. *ignes* (line 502)
   c. *Hecubam* and *Priamum* (line 501)
   d. *nurus* (line 501)

10. In line 505, *qua* is best translated
    a. with which
    b. where
    c. in which
    d. from where

11. In line 510, *nequiquam* and *inutile* emphasize
    a. Priam's age
    b. how Priam puts on his armor
    c. how the enemy defeats Priam
    d. the futility of Priam's efforts

12. Line 515 contains an example of
    a. apostrophe
    b. tmesis
    c. hiatus
    d. anastrophe

13. The case of *coniunx* (line 519) is
    a. nominative
    b. vocative
    c. accusative
    d. ablative

14. The verb *adforet* (line 522) is
    a. imperfect subjunctive in a contrary-to-fact condition
    b. pluperfect subjunctive in a contrary-to-fact condition
    c. present subjunctive in a future-less-vivid (should/would) condition
    d. imperfect subjunctive in a wish

15. In line 524, *moriere* is
    a. present infinitive
    b. singular imperative
    c. second person future indicative
    d. third person perfect indicative

Translation *Suggested time: 10 minutes*

Translate the following passage as literally as possible.

Instat vi patria Pyrrhus; nec claustra nec ipsi
custodes sufferre valent; labat ariete crebro
ianua, et emoti procumbunt cardine postes.
Fit via vi; rumpunt aditus primosque trucidant
immissi Danai et late loca milite complent.

Short Answer Questions

From lines 489–517, find, copy out, and give the line numbers for all words related to parents, offspring, or descendants in general.

____

____

____

____

____

____

Matching #1

1.	____ *lubrica* (line 474)	a.	superlative adjective
2.	____ *domus* (line 483)	b.	accusative plural noun
3.	____ *veterum* (line 484)	c.	present passive infinitive
4.	____ *penitus* (line 487)	d.	future indicative verb
5.	____ *aditus* (line 494)	e.	neuter plural adjective
6.	____ *procubuere* (line 505)	f.	genitive plural adjective
7.	____ *veterrima* (line 513)	g.	adverb
8.	____ *cingi* (line 520)	h.	perfect indicative verb
9.	____ *moriere* (line 524)	i.	ablative singular adjective
10.	____ *sacra* (line 525)	j.	nominative singular noun

Matching #2

1.	____ *Priami* (line 484)	a.	son of Priam and Hecuba
2.	____ *Neoptolemum* (line 500)	b.	Priam's wife
3.	____ *Atridas* (line 500)	c.	Pyrrhus
4.	____ *Hecubam* (line 501)	d.	King of Troy
5.	____ *Hector* (line 522)	e.	Menelaus and Agamemnon

Essay *Suggested time: 20 minutes*

If a movie of the *Aeneid* were being made, lines 476–517 could serve as clear directions for the camera person. What would the movement of the camera be? On what vignettes would it stop and linger? Choose and translate phrases from lines 476–517 that give these "directions." Present your response in a well-organized essay.

Support your assertions with references drawn from **throughout** lines 476–517. All Latin words must be copied or their line numbers provided, AND they must be translated or paraphrased closely enough so that it is clear you understand the Latin. It is your responsibility to convince your reader that you are basing your conclusions on the Latin text and not merely on a general recollection of the passage. Direct your answer to the question; do not merely summarize the passage. Please write your essay on a separate piece of paper.

Scansion

Scan the following lines.

exiit oppositasque evicit gurgite moles,

fertur in arva furens cumulo camposque per omnes

cum stabulis armenta trahit. vidi ipse furentem

caede Neoptolemum geminosque in limine Atridas,

vidi Hecubam centumque nurus Priamumque per aras

(lines 497–501)

Notes

LESSON 16: BOOK II. 526–566

Ecce autem elapsus Pyrrhi de caede Polites,
unus natorum Priami, per tela, per hostes
porticibus longis fugit et vacua atria lustrat
saucius. Illum ardens infesto vulnere Pyrrhus
insequitur, iam iamque manu tenet et premit hasta.
Ut tandem ante oculos evasit et ora parentum,
concidit ac multo vitam cum sanguine fudit.
Hic Priamus, quamquam in media iam morte tenetur,
non tamen abstinuit nec voci iraeque pepercit:
'At tibi pro scelere,' exclamat, 'pro talibus ausis
di, si qua est caelo pietas quae talia curet,
persolvant grates dignas et praemia reddant
debita, qui nati coram me cernere letum
fecisti et patrios foedasti funere vultus.
At non ille, satum quo te mentiris, Achilles
talis in hoste fuit Priamo; sed iura fidemque
supplicis erubuit corpusque exsangue sepulcro
reddidit Hectoreum meque in mea regna remisit.'
Sic fatus senior telumque imbelle sine ictu
coniecit, rauco quod protinus aere repulsum,
et summo clipei nequiquam umbone pependit.
Cui Pyrrhus: 'Referes ergo haec et nuntius ibis
Pelidae genitori. Illi mea tristia facta
degeneremque Neoptolemum narrare memento.
Nunc morere.' Hoc dicens altaria ad ipsa trementem
traxit et in multo lapsantem sanguine nati,
implicuitque comam laeva, dextraque coruscum
extulit ac lateri capulo tenus abdidit ensem.
Haec finis Priami fatorum, hic exitus illum
sorte tulit Troiam incensam et prolapsa videntem
Pergama, tot quondam populis terrisque superbum
regnatorem Asiae. Iacet ingens litore truncus,
avulsumque umeris caput et sine nomine corpus.
At me tum primum saevus circumstetit horror.
obstipui; subiit cari genitoris imago,
ut regem aequaevum crudeli vulnere vidi
vitam exhalantem, subiit deserta Creusa
et direpta domus et parvi casus Iuli.
Respicio et quae sit me circum copia lustro.
Deseruere omnes defessi, et corpora saltu
ad terram misere aut ignibus aegra dedere.

Comprehension Questions

1. Whose son is Pyrrhus, also called Neoptolemus? Whose son is Polites?

2. What does Pyrrhus do to Polites in lines 526–32?

3. How does line 531 show Pyrrhus as especially cruel?

4. When Aeneas first appears in the poem in Book 1, he exclaims,"*o terque quaterque beati,/ quis ante ora patrum Troiae sub moenibus altis/ contigit oppetere!*" How does the action of lines 529–43 correspond to Aeneas' prayer in Book 1—or does it?

5. In lines 535–43, Priam compares Pyrrhus to his father Achilles. Whom does Priam find more honorable? Why?

6. How do lines 544–46 reinforce the image of Priam seen in lines 507–11?

7. What is Pyrrhus' attitude as he speaks to Priam in lines 547–50?

8. What does Aeneas say Priam was witnessing as he died (lines 554–57)?

9. What prompts Aeneas to think of his own father?

Short Answer Questions

Indicate True or False.

1. ____ The phrase *unus natorum* (line 527) is in apposition to Polites.
2. ____ In line 529, *illum* refers to Pyrrhus.
3. ____ *hasta* in line 530 is ablative of means/instrument.
4. ____ In line 532, *ac* connects *concidit* and *fudit.*
5. ____ There are two elisions in line 533.
6. ____ *voci* (line 534) is dative because of *abstinuit.*
7. ____ In line 537, *persolvant* is subjunctive in a future-less-vivid (should/would) condition.
8. ____ *coram* (line 538) is an adverb.
9. ____ *funere* in line 539 is an infinitive.
10. ____ *satum [esse]* (line 540) has *te* as its subject.
11. ____ In line 542, *–que* connects *erubuit* and *reddidit.*
12. ____ The antecedent of *quod* (line 545) is *ictu.*
13. ____ The translation of *nequiquam* in line 546 is "uselessly."
14. ____ In line 547, *referes* is present subjunctive.
15. ____ *illi* (line 548) is an indirect object.
16. ____ In line 549, *memento* is an imperative.
17. ____ *morere* (line 550) is an imperative.
18. ____ The translation of *lapsantem sanguine nati* in line 551 is "the son slipping in blood."
19. ____ In line 553, *lateri* and *capulo* are in the same case.
20. ____ *exitus* (line 554) is the subject of *tulit.*
21. ____ In line 555, *videntem* modifies *Troiam.*
22. ____ *regnatorem* (line 557) is in apposition to *illum* (line 554).
23. ____ In line 559, *me* is ablative.
24. ____ *imago* in line 560 is best translated as "ghost."
25. ____ *exhalantem* (line 562) modifies *vitam.*
26. ____ *casus* is nominative in line 563.

27. ____ In line 564, *sit* is subjunctive in an indirect question.

28. ____ *me circum* (line 564) is an example of anastrophe.

29. ____ *saltu* (line 565) is a supine.

30. ____ *misere* in line 566 is an adverb.

Translation *Suggested time: 20 minutes*

Translate the following passage as literally as possible.

. . . Hoc dicens altaria ad ipsa trementem
traxit et in multo lapsantem sanguine nati,
implicuitque comam laeva, dextraque coruscum
extulit ac lateri capulo tenus abdidit ensem.
Haec finis Priami fatorum, hic exitus illum
sorte tulit Troiam incensam et prolapsa videntem
Pergama, tot quondam populis terrisque superbum
regnatorem Asiae.

Translation and Analysis Questions

Translate the Latin used in the question and then answer the question.

1. What theme is Vergil emphasizing by using the phrases *unus natorum* (line 527), *ora parentum* (line 531), *nati letum* (line 538), *satum* (line 540), *genitori* (line 548), *sanguine nati* (line 551) and *genitoris imago* (line 560)?

____

____

____

____

2. When Vergil writes *quamquam in media iam morte tenetur* (line 533), to whose death is he referring? How might he mean this phrase at two levels?

____

____

____

____

3. Priam poses the question *si qua est caelo pietas quae talia curet* (line 536). From what you have read of the poem so far, do you think this is the case or not? Why?

____

____

____

____

4. In Lines 541–43, Priam describes his encounter with Achilles after the death of Hector by saying *sed iura fidemque/ supplicis erubuit corpusque exsangue sepulcro/ reddidit Hectoreum meque in mea regna remisit.* How does this recall lines 483–84 from Book I in which Achilles' treatment of Hector's corpse is described as *ter circum Iliacos raptaverat Hectora muros/ exanimumque auro corpus vendebat Achilles?* How does the tone in each of these two passages differ?

____

____

____

____

____

____

____

5. What characteristic of Neoptolemus/Pyrrhus is highlighted by the use of the words *trementem* (line 550) and *lapsantem sanguine nati* (line 551)?

6. As Priam dies, what else is Vergil emphasizing with the phrases *Troiam incensam* (line 555) and *prolapsa Pergama* (lines 555–56)? How might the phrases *ingens truncus* (line 557), *avulsum caput* (line 558) and *sine nomine corpus* (line 558) be read in two different ways?

7. A standard feature of epic poetry is a description of a hero's *aristeia,* his "display of glory on the battlefield," and Vergil does in fact include several passages of this sort later in the poem. How do lines 560–63, *subiit cari genitoris imago,/ ut regem aequaevum crudeli vulnere vidi/ vitam exhalantem, subiit deserta Creusa/ et direpta domus et parvi casus Iuli,* focus the reader's attention on a contrasting vision of war?

8. How do lines 565–66, *deseruere omnes defessi, et corpora saltu/ ad terram misere aut ignibus aegra dedere,* show yet another contrast with the concept of *aristeia*?

Essay *Suggested time: 20 minutes*

One of Vergil's themes in the *Aeneid* is the inversion of the natural order of things by war, i.e., children die before their parents. How does this passage emphasize this theme? Present your response in a well-organized essay.

Support your assertions with references drawn from **throughout** the passage. All Latin words must be copied or their line numbers provided, AND they must be translated or paraphrased closely enough so that it is clear you understand the Latin. It is your responsibility to convince your reader that you are basing your conclusions on the Latin text and not merely on a general recollection of the passage. Direct your answer to the question; do not merely summarize the passage. Please write your essay on a separate piece of paper.

Scansion

Scan the following lines.

Ut tandem ante oculos evasit et ora parentum,

concidit ac multo vitam cum sanguine fudit.

Hic Priamus, quamquam in media iam morte tenetur,

non tamen abstinuit nec voci iraeque pepercit:

(lines 531–34)

Notes

LESSON 17: BOOK II. 735–804

Hic mihi nescio quod trepido male numen amicum
confusam eripuit mentem. namque avia cursu
dum sequor et nota excedo regione viarum,
heu misero coniunx fatone erepta Creusa
substitit, erravitne via seu lapsa resedit,
incertum; nec post oculis est reddita nostris.
Nec prius amissam respexi animumve reflexi
quam tumulum antiquae Cereris sedemque sacratam
venimus: hic demum collectis omnibus una
defuit, et comites natumque virumque fefellit.
Quem non incusavi amens hominumque deorumque,
aut quid in eversa vidi crudelius urbe?
Ascanium Anchisenque patrem Teucrosque penates
commendo sociis et curva valle recondo;
ipse urbem repeto et cingor fulgentibus armis.
Stat casus renovare omnes omnemque reverti
per Troiam et rursus caput obiectare periclis.
Principio muros obscuraque limina portae,
qua gressum extuleram, repeto et vestigia retro
observata sequor per noctem et lumine lustro:
horror ubique animo, simul ipsa silentia terrent.
Inde domum, si forte pedem, si forte tulisset,
me refero: inruerant Danai et tectum omne tenebant.
Ilicet ignis edax summa ad fastigia vento
volvitur; exsuperant flammae, furit aestus ad auras.
Procedo et Priami sedes arcemque reviso:
et iam porticibus vacuis Iunonis asylo
custodes lecti Phoenix et dirus Ulixes
praedam adservabant. Huc undique Troia gaza
incensis erepta adytis, mensaeque deorum
crateresque auro solidi, captivaque vestis
congeritur. Pueri et pavidae longo ordine matres
stant circum.
Ausus quin etiam voces iactare per umbram
implevi clamore vias, maestusque Creusam
nequiquam ingeminans iterumque iterumque vocavi.
Quaerenti et tectis urbis sine fine ruenti
infelix simulacrum atque ipsius umbra Creusae
visa mihi ante oculos et nota maior imago.
Obstipui, steteruntque comae et vox faucibus haesit.
Tum sic adfari et curas his demere dictis:
'Quid tantum insano iuvat indulgere dolori,

o dulcis coniunx? Non haec sine numine divum
eveniunt; nec te comitem hinc portare Creusam
fas, aut ille sinit superi regnator Olympi.
Longa tibi exsilia et vastum maris aequor arandum,
et terram Hesperiam venies, ubi Lydius arva
inter opima virum leni fluit agmine Thybris.
Illic res laetae regnumque et regia coniunx
parta tibi; lacrimas dilectae pelle Creusae.
Non ego Myrmidonum sedes Dolopumve superbas
aspiciam aut Grais servitum matribus ibo,
Dardanis et divae Veneris nurus;
sed me magna deum genetrix his detinet oris.
Iamque vale et nati serva communis amorem.'
Haec ubi dicta dedit, lacrimantem et multa volentem
dicere deseruit, tenuesque recessit in auras.
ter conatus ibi collo dare bracchia circum;
ter frustra comprensa manus effugit imago,
par levibus ventis volucrique simillima somno.
Sic demum socios consumpta nocte reviso.
Atque hic ingentem comitum adfluxisse novorum
invenio admirans numerum, matresque virosque,
collectam exsilio pubem, miserabile vulgus.
Undique convenere animis opibusque parati
in quascumque velim pelago deducere terras.
Iamque iugis summae surgebat Lucifer Idae
ducebatque diem, Danaique obsessa tenebant
limina portarum, nec spes opis ulla dabatur.
Cessi et sublato montes genitore petivi.

Comprehension Questions

1. In lines 738–40, Aeneas explains why he has said that some divine power has "snatched away my confused mind." What is the reason?

____

____

2. To what place had Aeneas and his comrades come before he noticed that Creusa was missing?

____

____

3. Whom or what does Aeneas say he takes care of before he returns to the city to search for Creusa?

____

____

4. What does Aeneas say he found terrifying when he entered the city?

5. Identify and give the line numbers of at least three places that Aeneas specifically says he visited to search for Creusa.

6. What was the state of Aeneas' home when he saw it?

7. What were Phoenix and Ulysses guarding in Juno's temple?

8. What is Aeneas' reaction when Creusa's ghost first appears to him?

9. In lines 776–79, how does Creusa console Aeneas?

10. What does Creusa prophesy to Aeneas in lines 780–84?

11. What alternate fate does Creusa feel grateful she will avoid?

12. What is Creusa's final injunction to Aeneas?

13. Lines 792–93 are particularly heart-rending. Why?

14. To what does Aeneas liken Creusa's departing ghost?

15. How does Aeneas describe the group of refugees?

16. What time is it when Aeneas begins to lead the refugees on their journey? What is the significance of that time?

17. What is Vergil emphasizing with the final line of Book II?

Multiple Choice Questions *Suggested time: 25 minutes*

1. The word that *nescio quod* (line 735) modifies is
   a. *amicum* (line 735)
   b. *male* (line 735)
   c. *mentem* (line 736)
   d. *numen* (line 735)

2. The best translation of *post* in line 740 is
   a. behind
   b. after
   c. before
   d. afterward

3. In line 743, *una* is
   a. a nominative adjective modifying Ceres (understood)
   b. a nominative adjective modifying Creusa (understood)
   c. an adverb
   d. an ablative adjective with *defuit*

4. In line 744, *virum* refers to
   a. Aeneas
   b. Anchises
   c. Ascanius
   d. Priam

5. The form of *crudelius* (line 746) is
   a. positive nominative singular masculine adjective
   b. comparative nominative singular neuter adjective
   c. comparative accusative singular neuter adjective
   d. comparative adverb

6. In line 749, *ipse* refers to
   a. Teucer (understood)
   b. Ascanius
   c. Anchises
   d. Aeneas

7. Line 749 contains an example of
   a. hysteron proteron
   b. hyperbole
   c. hendiadys
   d. hyperbaton

8. The part of speech of *rursus* (line 751) is
   a. noun
   b. adjective
   c. adverb
   d. participle

9. In line 754, *observata* modifies
   a. *limina* (line 752)
   b. *vestigia* (line 753)
   c. *noctem* (line 754)
   d. *lumine* (line 754)

10. From lines 763–66 (*huc . . . congeritur*), we learn that
    a. the Trojan treasures have been burnt by the Greeks
    b. the Greeks are holding captives
    c. the Trojans have gathered treasure as a ransom
    d. the Greeks have plundered the Trojan temples

11. The number of elisions in line 770 is
    a. zero
    b. one
    c. two
    d. three

12. From lines 772–73 (*infelix . . . imago*), we learn that
    a. Creusa's ghost appears larger than life
    b. the statue has brought bad luck
    c. the shade prevents Aeneas from seeing Creusa
    d. the ghost appeared larger than life to Creusa

13. The form of *demere* (line 775) is
    a. perfect indicative
    b. present imperative
    c. future indicative
    d. present infinitive

14. In line 776, *quid* is translated
    a. what
    b. why
    c. which
    d. how

15. Line 777 contains an example of
    a. chiasmus
    b. litotes
    c. apostrophe
    d. anastrophe

16. In line 779, *regnator* refers to
    a. Aeneas
    b. Jupiter
    c. Priam
    d. Agamemnon

17. The subject of *fluit* (line 782) is
    a. *arva* (line 781)
    b. *Lydius* (line 781)
    c. *Thybris* (line 782)
    d. *opima* (line 782)

18. The part of speech of *servitum* (line 786) is
    a. adjective
    b. noun
    c. participle
    d. supine

19. In line 789, *et* connects
    a. *vale* and *serva*
    b. *vale* and *nati*
    c. *iamque* and *serva*
    d. *vale* and *communis*

20. The word that *lacrimantem* (line 790) modifies is
    a. Creusa (understood)
    b. Aeneas (understood)
    c. *volentem* (line 790)
    d. *amorem* (line 789)

21. The case and number of *manus* (line 793) is
    a. nominative singular
    b. accusative plural
    c. nominative plural
    d. genitive singular

22. In lines 796–98 (*Atque . . . vulgus*), we learn that
    a. the mothers and men found the crowd miserable
    b. no one is ready for the exile to come
    c. Aeneas is surprised by the number of people
    d. the comrades had gathered women and children and prepared them for exile

23. The place name *Idae* (line 801) is near
    a. Olympus
    b. Rome
    c. Carthage
    d. Troy

Translation *Suggested time: 10 minutes*

Translate the following passage as literally as possible.

Longa tibi exsilia et vastum maris aequor arandum,
et terram Hesperiam venies, ubi Lydius arva
inter opima virum leni fluit agmine Thybris.
Illic res laetae regnumque et regia coniunx
parta tibi; lacrimas dilectae pelle Creusae.

____

____

____

____

____

____

Short Answer Questions

From lines 735–59, find, copy out, and provide line references in parentheses for:

1. two pluperfect indicative verbs ______________________
2. three infinitives ______________________
3. two nominative adjectives that modify a first person subject ______________________
4. a pluperfect subjunctive verb ______________________

5. sixteen first person singular verbs ______________________________

____

____

____

6. four references to divinities/religion ______________________________

____

7. two perfect participles in the nominative, singular, feminine ______________________________

From lines 760–84, find, copy out, and provide line references in parentheses for:

8. three present participles ______________________________

____

9. a passive periphrastic ______________________________

10. an ablative of comparison ______________________________

11. an imperative verb ______________________________

12. a dative of agent ______________________________

13. a noun in the vocative ______________________________

From lines 785–804, find, copy out, and provide line references in parentheses for:

14. two verbs in the future tense ______________________________

15. two ablatives absolute ______________________________

16. three present participles ______________________________

____

17. a third person perfect active indicative verb ending in *–ere* ______________________________

18. three present indicative verbs ______________________________

19. a second declension genitive plural ending in *–um* ______________________________

20. a noun in apposition to a pronoun ______________________________

Essay *Suggested time: 20 minutes*

How does Aeneas feel about Creusa? Present your response in a well-organized essay.

Support your assertions with references drawn from **throughout** lines 735–794. All Latin words must be copied or their line numbers provided, AND they must be translated or paraphrased closely enough so that it is clear you understand the Latin. It is your responsibility to convince your reader that you are basing your conclusions on the Latin text and not merely on a general recollection of the passage. Direct your answer to the question; do not merely summarize the passage. Please write your essay on a separate piece of paper.

Scansion

Scan the following lines.

principio muros obscuraque limina portae,

qua gressum extuleram, repeto et vestigia retro

observata sequor per noctem et lumine lustro:

horror ubique animo, simul ipsa silentia terrent.

(lines 752–55)

Book II Comprehensive Review Essay

One of the themes Vergil explores in the *Aeneid* is how war destroys the innocent, i.e., those who are not actually battling. Drawing on episodes throughout Book II, show how Vergil presents this idea through both the characters he focuses on and the setting. Present your response in a well-organized essay. Please write your essay on a separate piece of paper.

THE *AENEID* BOOK IV SELECTIONS WITH EXERCISES

LESSON 18: BOOK IV. 1–64

At regina gravi iamdudum saucia cura
vulnus alit venis et caeco carpitur igni.
Multa viri virtus animo multusque recursat
gentis honos; haerent infixi pectore vultus
verbaque nec placidam membris dat cura quietem.
Postera Phoebea lustrabat lampade terras
umentemque Aurora polo dimoverat umbram,
cum sic unanimam adloquitur male sana sororem:
"Anna soror, quae me suspensam insomnia terrent!
Quis novus hic nostris successit sedibus hospes,
quem sese ore ferens, quam forti pectore et armis!
Credo equidem, nec vana fides, genus esse deorum.
Degeneres animos timor arguit. Heu, quibus ille
iactatus fatis! Quae bella exhausta canebat!
Si mihi non animo fixum immotumque sederet
ne cui me vinclo vellem sociare iugali,
postquam primus amor deceptam morte fefellit;
si non pertaesum thalami taedaeque fuisset,
huic uni forsan potui succumbere culpae.
Anna (fatebor enim) miseri post fata Sychaei
coniugis et sparsos fraterna caede penates
solus hic inflexit sensus animumque labantem
impulit. Agnosco veteris vestigia flammae.
Sed mihi vel tellus optem prius ima dehiscat
vel pater omnipotens adigat me fulmine ad umbras,
pallentes umbras Erebo noctemque profundam,
ante, pudor, quam te violo aut tua iura resolvo.
Ille meos, primus qui me sibi iunxit, amores
abstulit; ille habeat secum servetque sepulcro."
Sic effata sinum lacrimis implevit obortis.
Anna refert: "O luce magis dilecta sorori,
solane perpetua maerens carpere iuventa
nec dulces natos Veneris nec praemia noris?
Id cinerem aut manes credis curare sepultos?
Esto: aegram nulli quondam flexere mariti,
non Libyae, non ante Tyro; despectus Iarbas
ductoresque alii, quos Africa terra triumphis
dives alit: placitone etiam pugnabis amori?
Nec venit in mentem quorum consederis arvis?
Hinc Gaetulae urbes, genus insuperabile bello,
et Numidae infreni cingunt et inhospita Syrtis;
hinc deserta siti regio lateque furentes

Barcaei. Quid bella Tyro surgentia dicam
germanique minas?
Dis equidem auspicibus reor et Iunone secunda
hunc cursum Iliacas vento tenuisse carinas.
Quam tu urbem, soror, hanc cernes, quae surgere regna
coniugio tali! Teucrum comitantibus armis
Punica se quantis attollet gloria rebus!
Tu modo posce deos veniam, sacrisque litatis
indulge hospitio causasque innecte morandi,
dum pelago desaevit hiems et aquosus Orion,
quassataeque rates, dum non tractabile caelum."
His dictis impenso animum flammavit amore
spemque dedit dubiae menti solvitque pudorem.
Principio delubra adeunt pacemque per aras
exquirunt; mactant lectas de more bidentes
legiferae Cereri Phoeboque patrique Lyaeo,
Iunoni ante omnes, cui vincla iugalia curae.
Ipsa tenens dextra pateram pulcherrima Dido
candentis vaccae media inter cornua fundit,
aut ante ora deum pinguis spatiatur ad aras,
instauratque diem donis, pecudumque reclusis
pectoribus inhians spirantia consulit exta.

Comprehension Questions

1. The phrases *saucia* and *carpitur igni* (lines 1–2) do not describe Dido literally. What does Vergil mean by these phrases? ____________________

____

2. Why does Vergil describe Dido as *male sana* (line 8)? ____________________

____

3. With what aspects of Aeneas is Dido impressed? ____________________

____

4. Why does Dido feel that she does not want to fall in love with Aeneas? ____________________

____

____

5. What does Dido mean by *huic uni culpae* (line 19)? ____________________

____

6. What does Dido mean by the phrase *veteris vestigia flammae* (line 23)? ____________________

____

7. What does Dido say she would rather have happen than that she break the vow she has made to herself?

____

____

8. What arguments does Anna use to convince Dido that she should heed her feelings for Aeneas?

____

____

____

____

9. What is ironic about lines 45–49? ____

____

10. In line 54, how does Vergil reinforce the image of love as a flame? ______________________

____

11. Why does Dido especially pray to Juno? ____

____

Short Answer Questions

Complete the statement or answer the question.

1. *multus* (line 3) modifies ______________________

2. *–que* in line 5 connects ______________________ and ______________________

3. In line 8, *male sana* is an example of the rhetorical device ______________________

4. The case of *sese* (line 11) is ______________________

5. Although it is in a mixed condition, *sederet* (line 15) represents a subjunctive in the protasis ("if clause") of what type of condition? ______________________

6. *huic uni* (line 19) modifies ______________________

7. The case of *sensus* (line 22) is ______________________

8. The subject of *dehiscat* (line 24) is ______________________

9. *te* (line 27) refers to ______________________

10. In line 28, *ille* refers to ______________________

11. The case and case use of *luce* (line 31) is ______________________________________

12. *sorori* (line 31) refers to ____________________________

13. The tense and mood of *noris* (line 33) is____

14. The case of *Libyae* in line 36 is ____________________________

15. In line 38, *dives* modifies ____________________________

16. *genus* (line 40) is in apposition to ____________________________

17. *dicam* in line 43 is in the subjunctive because ____________________________

18. In line 46, *tenuisse* is in the infinitive because ____________________________

19. The mood and tense of *cernes* (line 47) is ____

20. The form of *veniam* (line 50) is ____

21. The part of speech of *morandi* (line 51) is ____________________________

22. *impenso* (line 54) modifies ____________________________

23. The case and use of *menti* (line 55) is ____________________________

24. *Lyaeo* (line 58) is another name for ____________________________

25. The object of *tenens* (line 60) is ____________________________

26. The subject of *consulit* (line 64) is ____________________________

Translation *Suggested time: 10 minutes*

Translate the following passage as literally as possible.

Si mihi non animo fixum immotumque sederet
ne cui me vinclo vellem sociare iugali,
postquam primus amor deceptam morte fefellit;
si non pertaesum thalami taedaeque fuisset,
huic uni forsan potui succumbere culpae.

____

____

____

____

____

____

Translation and Analysis Questions

Translate the Latin used in the question and answer the question.

1. In the phrase *caeco carpitur igni* (line 2), why is the *ignis* described as *caecus*?__________________

2. The ancient commentator Varro explained the use of the word *cura* (lines 1 and 5) by what he thought was its etymology in the combination of two words: *"cura quod cor urit"* (*'cura'* because it burns the heart). Find all instances in the passage where Vergil uses flame or fire to describe Dido's love. Provide line references in parentheses for your Latin choices.

3. The noun *culpae* (line 19) comes as a surprise at the end of the line. Until then, the reader is led to expect that *huic uni* (line 19) refers to Aeneas. How might both be true? ________________

4. When Dido says, *"ante, pudor, quam te violo aut tua iura resolvo"* (line 27), what is the effect of the apostrophe? ________________

5. When Anna asks, *"Id cinerem aut manes credis curare sepultos"* (line 34), to what does *id* refer? What is her point in asking this question? ________________

6. Anna advises Dido, *causasque innecte morandi* (line 51). How does she suggest that Dido use natural phenomena to keep Aeneas at Carthage? ________________

7. How does the phrase *solvitque pudorem* (line 55) correspond to line 27? ______________________

____

____

____

8. With the phrase *cui vincla iugalia curae* (line 59) Vergil emphasizes Dido's hopes. What is it that she wants to happen? ____

____

____

____

Essay *Suggested time: 20 minutes*

In lines 9–29, Dido expresses her emotional upheaval both by what she says and how she says it. What are her feelings? How does her method of expressing herself reinforce what she is saying? Present your response in a well-organized essay.

Support your assertions with references drawn from **throughout** this passage (lines 9–29 only). All Latin words must be copied or their line numbers provided, AND they must be translated or paraphrased closely enough so that it is clear you understand the Latin. It is your responsibility to convince your reader that you are basing your conclusions on the Latin text and not merely on a general recollection of the passage. Direct your answer to the question; do not merely summarize the passage. Please write your essay on a separate piece of paper.

Scansion

Scan the following lines.

abstulit; ille habeat secum servetque sepulcro (line 29)

hunc cursum Iliacas vento tenuisse carinas (line 46)

indulge hospitio causasque innecte morandi (line 51)

LESSON 19: BOOK IV. 65–128

Heu, vatum ignarae mentes! Quid vota furentem,
quid delubra iuvant? Est molles flamma medullas
interea et tacitum vivit sub pectore vulnus.
Uritur infelix Dido totaque vagatur
urbe furens, qualis coniecta cerva sagitta,
quam procul incautam nemora inter Cresia fixit
pastor agens telis liquitque volatile ferrum
nescius: illa fuga silvas saltusque peragrat
Dictaeos; haeret lateri letalis harundo.
Nunc media Aenean secum per moenia ducit
Sidoniasque ostentat opes urbemque paratam,
incipit effari mediaque in voce resistit;
nunc eadem labente die convivia quaerit,
Iliacosque iterum demens audire labores
exposcit pendetque iterum narrantis ab ore.
Post ubi digressi, lumenque obscura vicissim
luna premit suadentque cadentia sidera somnos,
sola domo maeret vacua stratisque relictis
incubat. Illum absens absentem auditque videtque,
aut gremio Ascanium genitoris imagine capta
detinet, infandum si fallere possit amorem.
Non coeptae adsurgunt turres, non arma iuventus
exercet portusve aut propugnacula bello
tuta parant: pendent opera interrupta minaeque
murorum ingentes aequataque machina caelo.
    Quam simul ac tali persensit peste teneri
cara Iovis coniunx nec famam obstare furori,
talibus adgreditur Venerem Saturnia dictis:
"Egregiam vero laudem et spolia ampla refertis
tuque puerque tuus (magnum et memorabile numen),
una dolo divum si femina victa duorum est.
Nec me adeo fallit veritam te moenia nostra
suspectas habuisse domos Karthaginis altae.
Sed quis erit modus, aut quo nunc certamine tanto?
Quin potius pacem aeternam pactosque hymenaeos
exercemus? Habes tota quod mente petisti:
ardet amans Dido traxitque per ossa furorem.
Communem hunc ergo populum paribusque regamus
auspiciis; liceat Phrygio servire marito
dotalisque tuae Tyrios permittere dextrae."
    Olli (sensit enim simulata mente locutam,
quo regnum Italiae Libycas averteret oras)

sic contra est ingressa Venus: "Quis talia demens
abnuat aut tecum malit contendere bello?
Si modo quod memoras factum fortuna sequatur.
Sed fatis incerta feror, si Iuppiter unam
esse velit Tyriis urbem Troiaque profectis,
miscerive probet populos aut foedera iungi.
Tu coniunx, tibi fas animum temptare precando.
Perge, sequar." Tum sic excepit regia Iuno:
"Mecum erit iste labor. Nunc qua ratione quod instat
confieri possit, paucis (adverte) docebo.
Venatum Aeneas unaque miserrima Dido
in nemus ire parant, ubi primos crastinus ortus
extulerit Titan radiisque retexerit orbem.
His ego nigrantem commixta grandine nimbum,
dum trepidant alae saltusque indagine cingunt,
desuper infundam et tonitru caelum omne ciebo.
Diffugient comites et nocte tegentur opaca:
speluncam Dido dux et Troianus eandem
devenient. adero et, tua si mihi certa voluntas,
conubio iungam stabili propriamque dicabo.
Hic hymenaeus erit." Non adversata petenti
adnuit atque dolis risit Cytherea repertis.

Comprehension Questions

1. In lines 65–68, Vergil continues his use of flame as an image for love. With what words does he do this? ______________________________

____

____

2. How does the simile in lines 69–73 illuminate Dido's emotional state? Who or what does the *pastor* (line 71) represent? ______________________________

____

____

3. Compare the result of Dido's love in lines 86–89 with Anna's prediction in lines 47–49.

____

____

____

4. How does Juno attempt to insult Venus in lines 93–95? ______________________________

____

____

5. What plan do the two goddesses seem to agree on in lines 102–12? ______________________

____

____

6. What outcome might the goddesses' two different views of the plan foreshadow? ____________

____

____

____

7. Earlier in the poem, terrible events often happened in the dark. How does Vergil continue the negative connotation of darkness with line 123? ______________________________

____

____

____

8. Juno says in line 126 exactly what she said in Book I.73. What was the situation then? What conclusion might we draw from the line's repetition here? ______________________

____

____

____

____

9. Find all the words in this passage formed from the *fur-* stem and give their line numbers.

____

____

____

Multiple Choice Questions *Suggested time: 30 minutes*

1. Vergil is suggesting in lines 65–66 (*heu . . . iuvant*) that
   a. prayers can aid a raging person
   b. although seers are ignorant, they can be helpful
   c. even sacred rites cannot help a person in love
   d. a person raging with love should go to shrines for help

2. In line 66, *est* is translated
   a. is
   b. was
   c. ate
   d. eats

3. The word that *tacitum* (line 67) modifies is
   a. *vulnus* (line 67)
   b. *flamma* (line 66)
   c. *pectore* (line 67)
   d. *vivit* (line 67)

4. In line 72, *nescius* modifies
   a. *Cresia* (line 70)
   b. *pastor* (line 71)
   c. *ferrum* (line 71)
   d. *quam* (line 70)

5. The case of *harundo* (line 73) is
   a. nominative
   b. dative
   c. ablative
   d. accusative

6. In line 77, *eadem* modifies
   a. the understood subject of *quaerit*
   b. *labente*
   c. *die*
   d. *convivia*

7. The word that *cadentia* (line 81) modifies is
   a. *luna* (line 81)
   b. *sidera* (line 81)
   c. *sola* (line 82)
   d. *domo* (line 82)

8. In line 84, *genitoris* refers to
   a. Ascanius
   b. Anchises
   c. Aeneas
   d. Jupiter

9. The best translation of *peste* in line 90 is
   a. with the pest
   b. from the disease
   c. from the passion
   d. by love

10. In line 94, *puer* refers to
    a. Cupid
    b. Ascanius
    c. Aeneas
    d. Apollo

11. The tone with which the phrase *magnum et memorabile numen* (line 94) is spoken is
    a. respectful
    b. sarcastic
    c. loving
    d. gentle

12. The subject of *habuisse* (line 97) is
    a. *me* (line 96)
    b. *te* (line 96)
    c. *moenia* (line 96)
    d. *domos* (line 97)

13. The number of elisions in line 99 is
    a. zero
    b. one
    c. two
    d. three

14. In line 100, *habes tota quod mente petisti* is translated
    a. you have all that I sought in my mind
    b. you have everything that you sought in your mind
    c. you have in mind all that you sought
    d. you have what you sought with your whole mind

15. From lines 102–3 (*communem . . . auspiciis*) we learn that
    a. Dido and Aeneas will marry and create a common people
    b. Juno is proposing that the Carthaginians and the Trojans live together
    c. a common people should be ruled by favorable auspices
    d. we are guided as a nation by equal auspices

16. Lines 103–4 (*liceat . . . dextrae*) are best translated
    a. may it be allowed for Dido to serve a Trojan husband and to give the Carthagians as a dowry to your right hand
    b. may a Phrygian husband serve and submit a dowry to your right hand for the Tyrians
    c. she might have been permitted to serve a Phrygian husband and the Tyrians to give a dowry to your right hand
    d. it would have been permitted to serve a Phrygian husband and to give the Tyrians a dowry for your right hand

17. From lines 105–6 (*sensit . . . oras*), we learn that
    a. the two goddesses had spoken under the pretence of saving their respective favorite lands
    b. the kingdom of Italy would be kept from Libyan shores because of Juno's speech
    c. Juno felt that Venus had lied to avert the kingdom of Italy
    d. Venus knows that Juno was being deceptive in order to save Carthage

18. The subjunctive verb *malit* (line 108) is
    a. in an indirect question
    b. used deliberatively
    c. in a relative clause of purpose
    d. in an exhortation

19. In line 111, *–que* connects
    a. *Tyriis* and *profectis*
    b. *urbem* and *Troia*
    c. *velit* and *Tyriis*
    d. *esse* and *misceri*

20. The part of speech of *precando* (line 113) is
    a. gerundive
    b. gerund
    c. adjective
    d. adverb

21. In line 116, *possit* is subjunctive in a(n)
    a. relative clause of purpose
    b. future-less-vivid ("should/would") condition
    c. indirect question
    d. relative clause of characteristic

22. In line 117, *venatum* is a(n)
    a. perfect passive participle
    b. supine
    c. accusative noun
    d. perfect passive infinitive

23. *Titan* (line 119) is associated with
    a. war
    b. the moon
    c. rain
    d. the sun

24. The form of *infundam* (line 122) is
    a. accusative singular feminine noun
    b. accusative singular feminine gerundive
    c. future active indicative verb
    d. present active subjunctive verb

25. Another name for *Cytherea* (line 128) is
    a. Juno
    b. Dido
    c. Diana
    d. Venus

Translation *Suggested time: 15 minutes*

Translate the following passage as literally as possible.

"Mecum erit iste labor. Nunc qua ratione quod instat
confieri possit, paucis (adverte) docebo.
Venatum Aeneas unaque miserrima Dido
in nemus ire parant, ubi primos crastinus ortus
extulerit Titan radiisque retexerit orbem.
His ego nigrantem commixta grandine nimbum,
dum trepidant alae saltusque indagine cingunt,
desuper infundam et tonitru caelum omne ciebo.

Short Answer Questions

Matching #1

1.	____ *vota* (line 65)	a.	genitive singular participle
2.	____ *tota* (line 68)	b.	dative plural noun
3.	____ *nemora* (line 70)	c.	ablative singular adjective
4.	____ *telis* (line 71)	d.	accusative plural adjective
5.	____ *letalis* (line 73)	e.	nominative singular adjective
6.	____ *eadem* (line 77)	f.	nominative singular participle
7.	____ *narrantis* (line 79)	g.	nominative plural noun
8.	____ *stratis* (line 82)	h.	ablative plural noun
9.	____ *genitoris* (line 84)	i.	accusative plural noun
10.	____ *capta* (line 84)	j.	genitive singular noun

Matching #2

1.	____ *una* (line 95)	a.	present indicative
2.	____ *nostra* (line 96)	b.	present subjunctive
3.	____ *erit* (line 98)	c.	present infinitive
4.	____ *exercemus* (line 100)	d.	imperfect subjunctive
5.	____ *tota* (line 100)	e.	future indicative
6.	____ *ossa* (line 101)	f.	accusative plural noun
7.	____ *averteret* (line 106)	g.	ablative singular adjective
8.	____ *contra* (line 107)	h.	nominative singular adjective
9.	____ *abnuat* (line 108)	i.	accusative plural adjective
10.	____ *iungi* (line 112)	j.	adverb

Matching #3

1.	____ *precando* (line 113)	a.	adjective
2.	____ *tum* (line 114)	b.	adverb
3.	____ *adverte* (line 116)	c.	coordinating conjunction
4.	____ *in* (line 118)	d.	finite verb
5.	____ *ubi* (line 118)	e.	gerund
6.	____ *infundam* (line 122)	f.	imperative
7.	____ *speluncam* (line 124)	g.	noun
8.	____ *eandem* (line 124)	h.	participle
9.	____ *petenti* (line 127)	i.	preposition
10.	____ *atque* (line 128)	j.	subordinating conjunction

Essay *Suggested time: 20 minutes*

In lines 65–89, we see the symptoms of Dido's infatuation. How does Vergil show Dido's state of mind? Present your response in a well-organized essay.

Support your assertions with references drawn from **throughout** this passage (lines 65–89 only). All Latin words must be copied or their line numbers provided, AND they must be translated or paraphrased closely enough so that it is clear you understand the Latin. It is your responsibility to convince your reader that you are basing your conclusions on the Latin text and not merely on a general recollection of the passage. Direct your answer to the question; do not merely summarize the passage. Please write your essay on a separate piece of paper.

Scansion

Scan the following lines.

his ego nigrantem commixta grandine nimbum,

dum trepidant alae saltusque indagine cingunt,

desuper infundam et tonitru caelum omne ciebo.

(lines 120–22)

LESSON 20: BOOK IV. 129–197

Oceanum interea surgens Aurora reliquit.
It portis iubare exorto delecta iuventus,
retia rara, plagae, lato venabula ferro,
Massylique ruunt equites et odora canum vis.
Reginam thalamo cunctantem ad limina primi
Poenorum exspectant, ostroque insignis et auro
stat sonipes ac frena ferox spumantia mandit.
Tandem progreditur magna stipante caterva
Sidoniam picto chlamydem circumdata limbo;
cui pharetra ex auro, crines nodantur in aurum,
aurea purpuream subnectit fibula vestem.
Nec non et Phrygii comites et laetus Iulus
incedunt. Ipse ante alios pulcherrimus omnes
infert se socium Aeneas atque agmina iungit.
Qualis ubi hibernam Lyciam Xanthique fluenta
deserit ac Delum maternam invisit Apollo
instauratque choros, mixtique altaria circum
Cretesque Dryopesque fremunt pictique Agathyrsi;
ipse iugis Cynthi graditur mollique fluentem
fronde premit crinem fingens atque implicat auro,
tela sonant umeris: haud illo segnior ibat
Aeneas, tantum egregio decus enitet ore.
Postquam altos ventum in montes atque invia lustra,
ecce ferae saxi deiectae vertice caprae
decurrere iugis; alia de parte patentes
transmittunt cursu campos atque agmina cervi
pulverulenta fuga glomerant montesque relinquunt.
At puer Ascanius mediis in vallibus acri
gaudet equo iamque hos cursu, iam praeterit illos,
spumantemque dari pecora inter inertia votis
optat aprum, aut fulvum descendere monte leonem.
Interea magno misceri murmure caelum
incipit, insequitur commixta grandine nimbus,
et Tyrii comites passim et Troiana iuventus
Dardaniusque nepos Veneris diversa per agros
tecta metu petiere; ruunt de montibus amnes.
Speluncam Dido dux et Troianus eandem
deveniunt. Prima et Tellus et pronuba Iuno
dant signum; fulsere ignes et conscius aether
conubiis summoque ulularunt vertice Nymphae.
Ille dies primus leti primusque malorum
causa fuit; neque enim specie famave movetur

nec iam furtivum Dido meditatur amorem:
coniugium vocat, hoc praetexit nomine culpam.
Extemplo Libyae magnas it Fama per urbes,
Fama, malum qua non aliud velocius ullum:
mobilitate viget viresque adquirit eundo,
parva metu primo, mox sese attollit in auras
ingrediturque solo et caput inter nubila condit.
Illam Terra parens ira inritata deorum
extremam, ut perhibent, Coeo Enceladoque sororem
progenuit pedibus celerem et pernicibus alis,
monstrum horrendum, ingens, cui quot sunt corpore plumae,
tot vigiles oculi subter (mirabile dictu),
tot linguae, totidem ora sonant, tot subrigit aures.
Nocte volat caeli medio terraeque per umbram
stridens, nec dulci declinat lumina somno;
luce sedet custos aut summi culmine tecti
turribus aut altis, et magnas territat urbes,
tam ficti pravique tenax quam nuntia veri.
Haec tum multiplici populos sermone replebat
gaudens, et pariter facta atque infecta canebat:
venisse Aenean Troiano sanguine cretum,
cui se pulchra viro dignetur iungere Dido;
nunc hiemem inter se luxu, quam longa, fovere
regnorum immemores turpique cupidine captos.
Haec passim dea foeda virum diffundit in ora.
Protinus ad regem cursus detorquet Iarban
incenditque animum dictis atque aggerat iras.

Comprehension Questions

1. How does Vergil show the reader what time of day it is at the beginning of this passage?

____

____

2. In lines 134–39, what colors does Vergil emphasize? What aspect of Dido's position do they reinforce?

____

____

____

3. How does the simile in lines 143–150 develop Aeneas' character? ____________________

____

____

____

____

4. What aspect of Ascanius' character is emphasized in lines 156–59? ____________________

____

____

5. The description of the storm in lines 160–64 recalls what earlier passage in the poem?

____

____

6. How does Vergil employ natural phenomena to recreate a typical wedding ceremony?

____

____

____

7. What do lines 169–72 foreshadow? ____________________

____

____

8. In the personification of Fama (lines 173–90), Vergil gives one of the most vivid descriptions of a monster in ancient literature. Though Fama has a frightening appearance, its greatest destructiveness appears in lines 188–90. What is it that makes Fama so harmful?

____

____

____

____

Multiple Choice Questions *Suggested time: 20 minutes*

1. The case of *vis* (line 132) is
   a. nominative
   b. accusative

2. The phrase *magna stipante caterva* (line 136) is translated
   a. thronged by a great crowd
   b. with a great crowd thronging around

3. In line 142, *se* refers to
   a. Aeneas
   b. Iulus

4. Line 145 contains an example of
   a. apostrophe
   b. anastrophe

5. In line 147, *molli* modifies
   a. Cynthi
   b. fronde

6. The sentence *tantum egregio decus enitet ore* (line 150) is translated
   a. he shines from his noble face with such great dignity
   b. such great dignity shines forth from his noble face

7. In line 153, *decurrere* is
   a. perfect indicative
   b. present infinitive

8. The word *hos* (line 157) is the object of
   a. gaudet
   b. praeterit

9. In line 158, *dari* is
   a. an infinitive in indirect statement
   b. a complementary infinitive

10. The case of *commixta* (line 161) is
    a. nominative
    b. ablative

11. The phrase *Troiana iuventus Dardaniusque nepos Veneris* (lines 162–63) is translated
    a. the Dardanian youth from Troy and the grandson of Venus
    b. the Trojan youth and the Dardanian grandson of Venus

12. In line 170, *–ve* connects
    a. *fama* and *movetur*
    b. *specie* and *fama*

13. The case of *hoc* (line 172) is
    a. accusative
    b. ablative

14. In line 174, *qua* is
    a. ablative of means
    b. ablative of comparison

15. In line 174, *velocius* is
    a. masculine
    b. neuter

16. In line 178, *illam* is the object of
    a. *perhibent*
    b. *progenuit*

17. In line 181, *ingens* is
    a. neuter
    b. feminine

18. The case and number of *nuntia* (line 188) is
    a. nominative singular
    b. accusative plural

19. In line 193, *fovere* is
    a. an infinitive in indirect statement
    b. a complementary infinitive

20. The case of *virum* (line 195) is
    a. genitive
    b. accusative

Translation *Suggested time: 10 minutes*

Translate the following passage as literally as possible.

Extemplo Libyae magnas it Fama per urbes,
Fama, malum qua non aliud velocius ullum:
mobilitate viget viresque adquirit eundo,
parva metu primo, mox sese attollit in auras
ingrediturque solo et caput inter nubila condit.

____

____

____

____

____

____

Short Answer Questions

Matching

1.	____ Agathyrsi	a.	country in Asia Minor
2.	____ Aurora	b.	people of Crete
3.	____ Coeus	c.	mountain on Delos
4.	____ Cretes	d.	mother earth
5.	____ Cynthus	e.	country in North Africa
6.	____ Dardanius	f.	river near Troy
7.	____ Delos	g.	people of Northern Greece
8.	____ Dryopes	h.	Trojan
9.	____ Iarbas	i.	one of the sons of Earth
10.	____ Libya	j.	Apollo's island birthplace
11.	____ Lycia	k.	people of Scythia
12.	____ Tellus	l.	dawn
13.	____ Xanthus	m.	North African chieftan, suitor of Dido

Essay *Suggested time: 20 minutes*

How does Vergil create a sense of foreboding in lines 160–72? Present your response in a well-organized essay.

Support your assertions with references drawn from **throughout** this passage (lines 160–72 only). All Latin words must be copied or their line numbers provided, AND they must be translated or paraphrased closely enough so that it is clear you understand the Latin. It is your responsibility to convince your reader that you are basing your conclusions on the Latin text and not merely on a general recollection of the passage. Direct your answer to the question; do not merely summarize the passage. Please write your essay on a separate piece of paper.

Scansion

Scan the following lines.

deserit ac Delum maternam invisit Apollo

instauratque choros, mixtique altaria circum

Cretesque Dryopesque fremunt pictique Agathyrsi;

(lines 144–46)

Notes

LESSON 21: BOOK IV. 198–278

Hic Hammone satus rapta Garamantide nympha
templa Iovi centum latis immania regnis,
centum aras posuit vigilemque sacraverat ignem,
excubias divum aeternas, pecudumque cruore
pingue solum et variis florentia limina sertis.
Isque amens animi et rumore accensus amaro
dicitur ante aras media inter numina divum
multa Iovem manibus supplex orasse supinis:
"Iuppiter omnipotens, cui nunc Maurusia pictis
gens epulata toris Lenaeum libat honorem,
aspicis haec? An te, genitor, cum fulmina torques
nequiquam horremus, caecique in nubibus ignes
terrificant animos et inania murmura miscent?
Femina, quae nostris errans in finibus urbem
exiguam pretio posuit, cui litus arandum
cuique loci leges dedimus, conubia nostra
reppulit ac dominum Aenean in regna recepit.
Et nunc ille Paris cum semiviro comitatu,
Maeonia mentum mitra crinemque madentem
subnexus, rapto potitur: nos munera templis
quippe tuis ferimus famamque fovemus inanem."
Talibus orantem dictis arasque tenentem
audiit Omnipotens, oculosque ad moenia torsit
regia et oblitos famae melioris amantes.
Tum sic Mercurium adloquitur ac talia mandat:
"Vade age, nate, voca Zephyros et labere pennis
Dardaniumque ducem, Tyria Karthagine qui nunc
exspectat fatisque datas non respicit urbes,
adloquere et celeres defer mea dicta per auras.
Non illum nobis genetrix pulcherrima talem
promisit Graiumque ideo bis vindicat armis;
sed fore qui gravidam imperiis belloque frementem
Italiam regeret, genus alto a sanguine Teucri
proderet, ac totum sub leges mitteret orbem.
Si nulla accendit tantarum gloria rerum
nec super ipse sua molitur laude laborem,
Ascanione pater Romanas invidet arces?
Quid struit? Aut qua spe inimica in gente moratur
nec prolem Ausoniam et Lauinia respicit arva?
Naviget! Haec summa est, hic nostri nuntius esto."
Dixerat. Ille patris magni parere parabat
imperio; et primum pedibus talaria nectit

aurea, quae sublimem alis sive aequora supra
seu terram rapido pariter cum flamine portant.
Tum virgam capit: hac animas ille evocat Orco
pallentes, alias sub Tartara tristia mittit,
dat somnos adimitque, et lumina morte resignat.
Illa fretus agit ventos et turbida tranat
nubila. Iamque volans apicem et latera ardua cernit
Atlantis duri caelum qui vertice fulcit,
Atlantis, cinctum adsidue cui nubibus atris
piniferum caput et vento pulsatur et imbri,
nix umeros infusa tegit, tum flumina mento
praecipitant senis, et glacie riget horrida barba.
Hic primum paribus nitens Cyllenius alis
constitit; hinc toto praeceps se corpore ad undas
misit avi similis, quae circum litora, circum
piscosos scopulos humilis volat aequora iuxta.
Haud aliter terras inter caelumque volabat
litus harenosum ad Libyae, ventosque secabat
materno veniens ab avo Cyllenia proles.
Ut primum alatis tetigit magalia plantis,
Aenean fundantem arces ac tecta novantem
conspicit. Atque illi stellatus iaspide fulva
ensis erat Tyrioque ardebat murice laena
demissa ex umeris, dives quae munera Dido
fecerat, et tenui telas discreverat auro.
Continuo invadit: "Tu nunc Karthaginis altae
fundamenta locas pulchramque uxorius urbem
exstruis? Heu, regni rerumque oblite tuarum!
Ipse deum tibi me claro demittit Olympo
regnator, caelum et terras qui numine torquet,
ipse haec ferre iubet celeres mandata per auras:
quid struis? Aut qua spe Libycis teris otia terris?
Si te nulla movet tantarum gloria rerum
[nec super ipse tua moliris laude laborem,]
Ascanium surgentem et spes heredis Iuli
respice, cui regnum Italiae Romanaque tellus
debetur." Tali Cyllenius ore locutus
mortales visus medio sermone reliquit
et procul in tenuem ex oculis evanuit auram.

Comprehension Questions

1. Who are Iarbas' parents? ______

2. Why does Iarbas refer to Aeneas as *ille Paris* (line 215)? ______

3. In your opinion, is Iarbas angrier because he has lost Dido or because he has lost her kingdom? Copy out and translate at least one phrase to support your answer. ______

4. What is the tone of Iarbas' prayer in lines 206–18? What is he feeling? ______

5. To what two events is Jupiter referring when he says *bis vindicat* (line 228)? ______

6. After listing several reasons why Aeneas should linger no longer in Carthage, Jupiter gives a final one. What is it? ______

7. What two pieces of Mercury's equipment does Vergil mention? What power does each give Mercury?

8. What mountain does Vergil personify? How is it/he described? ______

9. To whom/what is Mercury compared in the simile in lines 253–55? ____________________

____

____

10. What is Aeneas wearing when Mercury sees him in lines 260–64? ____________________

____

____

11. Mercury repeats Jupiter's advice to Aeneas, but he adds emphasis in his mention of Ascanius. With what words does he do this? Provide line references in parentheses for your Latin choices.

____

____

____

____

Multiple Choice Questions *Suggested time: 15 minutes*

Choose the better translation.

1. *dicitur* (line 204)
   a. he is said
   b. it is said

2. *cui* (line 206)
   a. whose
   b. to whom

3. *arandum* (line 212)
   a. must be plowed
   b. to be plowed

4. *comitatu* (line 215)
   a. having been accompanied
   b. company

5. *mentum* (line 216)
   a. as to his chin
   b. of minds

6. *labere* (line 223)
   a. to glide
   b. glide

7. *fore* (line 229)
   a. will be
   b. would be

8. *gravidam imperiis belloque frementem/ Italiam* (lines 229–30)
   a. Italy, heavy with arms and war, and raging
   b. Italy, heavy with arms and raging with war

9. *aut qua spe inimica in gente moratur* (line 235)
   a. or with what hostile hope is he lingering among the people
   b. or with what hope is he lingering among the hostile people

10. *naviget* (line 237)
   a. let him sail
   b. he will sail

11. *alis* (line 240)
   a. than the others
   b. with wings

12. *Orco* (line 242)
   a. from Orcus
   b. to Orcus

13. *imbri* (line 249)
   a. by rain
   b. for rain

14. *glacie riget horrida barba* (line 251)
   a. (his) beard is stiff with rough ice
   b. (his) rough beard is stiff with ice

15. *nitens* (line 252)
   a. resting
   b. shining

16. *materno veniens ab avo* (line 258)
   a. coming from his mother's bird
   b. coming from his mother's ancestor

17. *dives quae munera Dido/ fecerat* (lines 263–64)
   a. which gifts rich Dido had made
   b. which rich gifts Dido had made

18. *oblite* (line 267)
   a. forget
   b. having forgotten

19. *aut qua spe Libycis teris otia terris* (line 271)
   a. in (your) hope what leisure are you wearing away in the Libyan lands
   b. with what hope are you wearing away (your) leisure in the Libyan lands

20. *cui* (line 275)
   a. by whom
   b. to whom

Translation *Suggested time: 15 minutes*

Translate the following passage as literally as possible.

Continuo invadit: "Tu nunc Karthaginis altae
fundamenta locas pulchramque uxorius urbem
exstruis? Heu, regni rerumque oblite tuarum!
Ipse deum tibi me claro demittit Olympo
regnator, caelum et terras qui numine torquet,
ipse haec ferre iubet celeres mandata per auras:
quid struis? Aut qua spe Libycis teris otia terris?

____

____

____

____

____

____

____

____

Short Answer Questions

From lines 198–231, find, copy out, and provide line references in parentheses for:

1. an ablative with a deponent verb ______________________
2. an example of chiasmus ______________________
3. a future infinitive ______________________
4. a line with four imperatives ______________________
5. an example of anaphora ______________________
6. a line with three elisions ______________________
7. two nouns in apposition to one another ______________________
8. a superlative adjective ______________________
9. an accusative, plural, feminine, perfect passive participle ______________________
10. an example of metonymy ______________________

From lines 232–58, find, copy out, and provide line references in parentheses for:

11. three examples of anastrophe ______________________________
12. a reflexive pronoun ______________________________
13. three present participles ______________________________
14. an imperative ______________________________
15. an example of synchysis ______________________________
16. a relative pronoun in the nominative, plural, neuter ______________________________
17. a perfect, passive participle in the nominative, singular, neuter ______________________________
18. a verb in the present subjunctive______________________________
19. *–que* connecting two accusative nouns______________________________
20. an example of anaphora ______________________________

From lines 259–78, find, copy out, and provide line references in parentheses for:

21. a participle in the vocative ______________________________
22. a line that begins with an adverb ______________________________
23. an example of chiasmus ______________________________
24. two verbs in the pluperfect tense______________________________
25. an example of two nominative nouns connected by *–que* ______________________________
26. a second declension genitive in *–um* ______________________________
27. a line with two prepositional phrases______________________________
28. a line with two present participles ______________________________
29. an interrogative pronoun ______________________________
30. two place names in the genitive______________________________

Essay *Suggested time: 20 minutes*

What is the tone of Jupiter's speech to Mercury in lines 223–37? What arguments does he say Mercury should use with Aeneas? Present your response in a well-organized essay.

Support your assertions with references drawn from **throughout** this passage (lines 223–37 only). All Latin words must be copied or their line numbers provided, AND they must be translated or paraphrased closely enough so that it is clear you understand the Latin. It is your responsibility to convince your reader that you are basing your conclusions on the Latin text and not merely on a general recollection of the passage. Direct your answer to the question; do not merely summarize the passage. Please write your essay on a separate piece of paper.

Scansion

Indicate whether or not each line is scanned properly.

1. __F__ **nēquī|quām hōr|rēmūs|, cāēcĭqu(e) ĭn |nūbĭbŭs |īgnēs** (line 209)
2. __F__ **rēgī|(a) ēt ōb|lītōs fă|māē mĕlĭ|ōrĭs ă|māntēs** (line 221)
3. __F__ **nēc prō|lēm Āu|sōnĭ(am) ĕt |Lāvĭniă |rēspĭcĭt |ārvă** (line 236)
4. __T__ **ūt prī|m(um) ālā|tīs tĕtĭ|gīt mā|gālĭă |plāntīs** (line 259)
5. __F__ **Āe nē|ān fūn|dānt(em) ār|cēs āc| tēctă nŏv|āntēm** (line 260)

LESSON 22: BOOK IV. 279–361

At vero Aeneas aspectu obmutuit amens,
arrectaeque horrore comae et vox faucibus haesit.
Ardet abire fuga dulcesque relinquere terras,
attonitus tanto monitu imperioque deorum.
Heu quid agat? Quo nunc reginam ambire furentem
audeat adfatu? Quae prima exordia sumat?
Atque animum nunc huc celerem nunc dividit illuc
in partisque rapit varias perque omnia versat.
Haec alternanti potior sententia visa est:
Mnesthea Sergestumque vocat fortemque Serestum,
classem aptent taciti sociosque ad litora cogant,
arma parent et quae rebus sit causa novandis
dissimulent; sese interea, quando optima Dido
nesciat et tantos rumpi non speret amores,
temptaturum aditus et quae mollissima fandi
tempora, quis rebus dexter modus. Ocius omnes
imperio laeti parent et iussa facessunt.
At regina dolos (quis fallere possit amantem?)
praesensit, motusque excepit prima futuros
omnia tuta timens. Eadem impia Fama furenti
detulit armari classem cursumque parari.
Saevit inops animi totamque incensa per urbem
bacchatur, qualis commotis excita sacris
Thyias, ubi audito stimulant trieterica Baccho
orgia nocturnusque vocat clamore Cithaeron.
Tandem his Aenean compellat vocibus ultro:
"Dissimulare etiam sperasti, perfide, tantum
posse nefas tacitusque mea decedere terra?
Nec te noster amor nec te data dextera quondam
nec moritura tenet crudeli funere Dido?
Quin etiam hiberno moliri sidere classem
et mediis properas Aquilonibus ire per altum,
crudelis? Quid, si non arva aliena domosque
ignotas peteres, et Troia antiqua maneret,
Troia per undosum peteretur classibus aequor?
Mene fugis? Per ego has lacrimas dextramque tuam te
(quando aliud mihi iam miserae nihil ipsa reliqui),
per conubia nostra, per inceptos hymenaeos,
si bene quid de te merui, fuit aut tibi quicquam
dulce meum, miserere domus labentis et istam,
oro, si quis adhuc precibus locus, exue mentem.
Te propter Libycae gentes Nomadumque tyranni

odere, infensi Tyrii; te propter eundem
exstinctus pudor et, qua sola sidera adibam,
fama prior. Cui me moribundam deseris hospes
(hoc solum nomen quoniam de coniuge restat)?
Quid moror? An mea Pygmalion dum moenia frater
destruat aut captam ducat Gaetulus Iarbas?
Saltem si qua mihi de te suscepta fuisset
ante fugam suboles, si quis mihi parvulus aula
luderet Aeneas, qui te tamen ore referret,
non equidem omnino capta ac deserta viderer."
Dixerat. Ille Iouis monitis immota tenebat
lumina et obnixus curam sub corde premebat.
Tandem pauca refert: "Ego te, quae plurima fando
enumerare vales, numquam, regina, negabo
promeritam, nec me meminisse pigebit Elissae
dum memor ipse mei, dum spiritus hos regit artus.
Pro re pauca loquar. Neque ego hanc abscondere furto
speravi (ne finge) fugam, nec coniugis umquam
praetendi taedas aut haec in foedera veni.
Me si fata meis paterentur ducere vitam
auspiciis et sponte mea componere curas,
urbem Troianam primum dulcesque meorum
reliquias colerem, Priami tecta alta manerent,
et recidiva manu posuissem Pergama victis.
Sed nunc Italiam magnam Gryneus Apollo,
Italiam Lyciae iussere capessere sortes;
hic amor, haec patria est. Si te Karthaginis arces
Phoenissam Libycaeque aspectus detinet urbis,
quae tandem Ausonia Teucros considere terra
invidia est? Et nos fas extera quaerere regna.
Me patris Anchisae, quotiens umentibus umbris
nox operit terras, quotiens astra ignea surgunt,
admonet in somnis et turbida terret imago;
me puer Ascanius capitisque iniuria cari,
quem regno Hesperiae fraudo et fatalibus arvis.
Nunc etiam interpres divum Iove missus ab ipso
(testor utrumque caput) celeres mandata per auras
detulit: ipse deum manifesto in lumine vidi
intrantem muros vocemque his auribus hausi.
Desine meque tuis incendere teque querelis;
Italiam non sponte sequor."

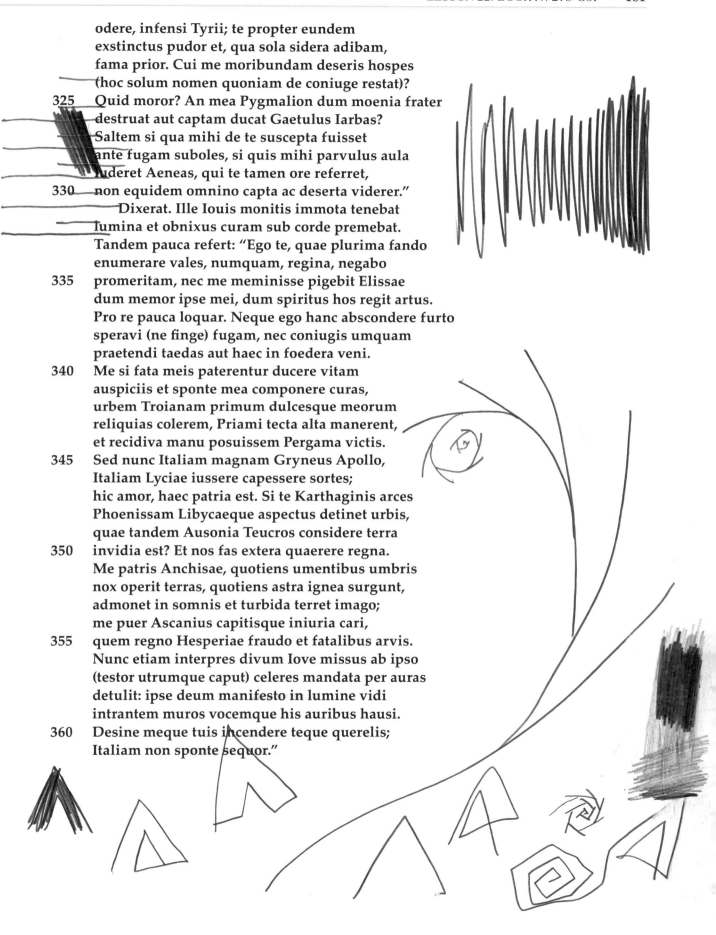

Comprehension Questions

1. How does Vergil emphasize Aeneas' divided feelings in lines 279–86? Provide line references and translate any words or phrases you use to support your answer.

2. Why does Aeneas tell his men to carry out his orders "silently" (line 289) and that they should "pretend otherwise" (line 291)?

3. How does Vergil explain Dido's awareness of Aeneas' plans? Identify at least two ways Vergil does his by writing out the relevant words or phrases and providing parenthetical line references for them.

4. Why does Vergil compare Dido to a Bacchante (lines 301–3)?

5. In her speech in lines 305–30, Dido begs Aeneas in several different ways not to leave. Paraphrase at least three of the reasons she does not want him to depart.

6. In response to Dido's distraught pleadings, Aeneas gives a remarkably logical list of reasons why he must do what he is doing. Paraphrase at least four of his points.

Multiple Choice Questions *Suggested time: 48 minutes*

1. The metrical pattern of the first four feet of line 280 is
   a. spondee-dactyl-dactyl-dactyl
   b. spondee-dactyl-spondee-dactyl
   c. spondee-spondee-dactyl-spondee
   d. spondee-spondee-dactyl-dactyl

2. In line 282, *monitu* is a(n)
   a. supine
   b. accusative singular noun
   c. ablative singular noun
   d. adverb

3. We learn from lines 285–86 (*atque . . . versat*) that
   a. Jupiter's command involved several parts
   b. Aeneas divided the work among his men
   c. Aeneas wanted Jupiter's command completed swiftly
   d. Aeneas had mixed feelings about what he had to do

4. In line 287, *alternanti* is best translated
   a. to him wavering
   b. for her changing
   c. of him alternating
   d. to her alternating

5. In line 289, *aptent* is present subjunctive in an implied
   a. indirect command
   b. result clause
   c. indirect question
   d. future-less-vivid condition

6. The case and part of speech of *novandis* (line 290) is
   a. ablative gerund
   b. dative gerund
   c. ablative gerundive
   d. dative gerundive

7. In line 291, *sese* refers to

a. Dido
b. Aeneas
c. Serestus
d. amores

8. The form of *sese* (line 291) is

a. ablative of means with *rumpi* (line 292)
b. accusative object of *temptaturum* (line 293)
c. accusative subject of of *temptaturum* (line 293)
d. accusative object of *nesciat* (line 292)

9. In line 294, *ocius* is

a. comparative adjective, accusative singular neuter
b. positive adverb
c. positive adjective, nominative singular masculine
d. comparative adverb

10. From lines 296–98 (*At . . . timens*), we learn that Dido

a. sensed everything ahead of time
b. feared even those things she did not need to
c. had planned to deceive her lover first
d. was fearful of any future movements

11. In line 298, *eadem* modifies

a. *prima* (line 297)
b. *omnia* (line 298)
c. *Fama* (line 298)
d. *classem* (line 299)

12. The metrical pattern of the first four feet of line 302 is

a. dactyl-spondee-dactyl-dactyl
b. spondee-dactyl-dactyl-dactyl
c. dactyl-dactyl-dactyl-dactyl
d. spondee-spondee-dactyl-dactyl

13. In line 302, *Thyias* is a name for

a. Bacchus
b. a worshipper of Bacchus
d. a place where Bacchus is worshipped
d. Bacchus' mother

14. Lines 305–306 (*dissimulare . . . terra*) are best translated

a. did you also hope to conceal treacherously so great a crime and be able to depart my land in silence
b. did not I also hope to conceal, treacherous one, such a great crime and that you would be able to depart my land silently
c. did I even hope that you would be able to conceal such a great wrongdoing, treacherous one, and depart, silent, from my land
d. did you even hope that you, treacherous one, were able to conceal such a great wrongdoing and to depart from my land silently

15. Lines 307–308 contain an example of
    a. aposiopesis
    b. anastrophe
    c. apostrophe
    d. anaphora

16. The future participle *moritura* (line 308) modifies
    a. *te* (line 307)
    b. *dextera* (line 307)
    c. *funere* (line 308)
    d. *Dido* (line 308)

17. In line 309, *sidere* is
    a. ablative
    b. adverb
    c. present imperative
    d. present infinitive

18. In lines 311–13 (*quid . . . aequor*) Dido argues that
    a. Aeneas should not seek unknown lands
    b. if Troy still stood, Aeneas would not seek foreign lands
    c. Aeneas would not sail through stormy waters even if he were going back to Troy
    d. by sailing to foreign lands, Aeneas is endangering his fleet

19. The best translation of *peteres* (line 312) is
    a. you were seeking
    b. you should seek
    c. you had sought
    d. you seek

20. In line 317, *quicquam* is
    a. accusative singular feminine
    b. nominative singular neuter
    c. accusative singular neuter
    d. dative singular masculine

21. Line 321 contains an example of
    a. anastrophe
    b. chiasmus
    c. synchysis
    d. hendiadys

22. In lines 320–21 (*te . . . Tyrii*) Dido claims that because of Aeneas
    a. the surrounding tribes and her own people hate her
    b. the Libyans are tyrants
    c. her own people are defenseless
    d. the Libyans hate the Nomads and the Tyrians hate Dido

23. In line 322, *sola* is
    a. ablative singular feminine
    b. nominative singular feminine
    c. accusative plural neuter
    d. nominative plural neuter

24. Dido in lines 323–24 (*cui . . . restat*) says that
    a. only her name is left to her
    b. Aeneas is now no longer her husband but an enemy
    c. she will now die because Aeneas is her enemy
    d. she can now call Aeneas only a guest and not a husband

25. In line 325, *dum* is translated
    a. when
    b. as long as
    c. until
    d. while

26. The antecedent of *qui* (line 329) is
    a. *ego* (understood)
    b. *mihi* (line 328)
    c. *Aeneas* (line 329)
    d. *parvulus* (line 328)

27. From lines 334–36 (*numquam . . . artus*), we learn that
    a. Aeneas will find Dido deserving when the spirit moves him
    b. as long as he is alive, Aeneas will find pleasure in remembering Dido
    c. as long as Aeneas is mindful, Dido will not control his feelings
    d. Aeneas will deny that he owes Dido anything as long as he is alive

28. *Elissae* (line 335) is
    a. dative with *promeritam*
    b. genitive with *meminisse*
    c. genitive with *pigebit*
    d. dative with *pigebit*

29. In line 343, *colerem* is subjunctive in
    a. an implied result clause
    b. the protasis ("if clause") of a present contrary-to-fact condition
    c. the apodosis ("then clause") of a present contrary-to-fact condition
    d. the apodosis ("then clause") of a past contrary-to-fact condition

30. Another name for *Pergama* (line 344) is
    a. Crete
    b. Rome
    c. Tyre
    d. Troy

31. In line 346, *sortes* is
    a. second person singular present active indicative
    b. nominative plural feminine
    c. second person singular present active subjunctive
    d. accusative singular neuter

32. Lines 347–48 (*si te . . . urbis*) are best translated
    a. if the view of Carthage and the Libyan city keep you at its citadel, a Phoenician one
    b. if the citadels of Carthage and the view of the Libyan city keep you, a Phoenician
    c. if the citadels keep you at Carthage and Libya and the views of the city, Phoenicia
    d. if the view of the Carthaginian citadels and of the city of Libya detain you, a Phoenician

33. *Ausonia terra* (line 349) is
    a. Tyre
    b. Italy
    c. Libya
    d. Greece

34. In line 349, *quae* modifies
    a. *urbis* (line 348)
    b. *Ausonia* (line 349)
    c. *terra* (line 349)
    d. *invidia* (line 350)

35. In line 354, *–que* connects
    a. *Ascanius* and *capitis*
    b. *Ascanius* and *cari*
    c. *puer* and *iniuria*
    d. *puer* and *cari*

36. Line 354 contains an example of
    a. polysyndeton
    b. synecdoche
    c. litotes
    d. enallage

37. In line 355, *fraudo* is
    a. ablative singular neuter
    b. first singular present active indicative
    c. dative singular neuter
    d. positive adverb

38. The number of elisions in line 355 is
    a. zero
    b. one
    c. two
    d. three

39. Aeneas says *testor utrumque caput* (line 357) because
    a. otherwise he will not have a witness
    b. Mercury was a witness
    c. he fears for his and his son's life
    d. he thinks Dido may not believe him

40. In line 358, *ipse* modifies
    a. *manifesto* line 358)
    b. *lumine* (line 358)
    c. *ego* (understood)
    d. *celeres* (line 357)

Translation *Suggested time: 20 minutes*

Translate the following passage as literally as possible.

Pro re pauca loquar. Neque ego hanc abscondere furto
speravi (ne finge) fugam, nec coniugis umquam
praetendi taedas aut haec in foedera veni.
Me si fata meis paterentur ducere vitam
auspiciis et sponte mea componere curas,
urbem Troianam primum dulcesque meorum
reliquias colerem, Priami tecta alta manerent,
et recidiva manu posuissem Pergama victis.

Short Answer Questions

Matching from lines 279–99

1.	____ accusative neuter plural	a.	*vero* (line 279)
2.	____ ablative of means	b.	*relinquere* (line 281)
3.	____ ablative of manner	c.	*iussa* (line 295)
4.	____ accusative plural masculine	d.	*fuga* (line 281)
5.	____ adverb	e.	*imperio* (line 282)
6.	____ complementary infinitive	f.	*motus* (line 297)
7.	____ gerund	g.	*modus* (line 294)
8.	____ gerundive	h.	*novandis* (line 290)
9.	____ infinitive in indirect statement	i.	*fandi* (line 293)
10.	____ nominative singular masculine	j.	*armari* (line 299)

Matching from lines 300–19

1.	____ *audito* (line 302)	a.	participle modifying a subject
2.	____ *data* (line 307)	b.	imperative
3.	____ *decedere* (line 306)	c.	vocative
4.	____ *dulce* (line 318)	d.	nominative adjective
5.	____ *hiberno* (line 309)	e.	participle in an ablative absolute
6.	____ *inceptos* (line 316)	f.	ablative
7.	____ *labentis* (line 318)	g.	participle modifying the object of a preposition
8.	____ *miserere* (line 318)	h.	adverb
9.	____ *perfide* (line 305)	i.	participle modifying a genitive object
10.	____ *ultro* (line 304)	j.	complementary infinitive

Matching from lines 320–39

1. ____ first person singular	a. *aula* (line 328)
2. ____ second person singular	b. *suboles* (line 328)
3. ____ third person plural	c. *artus* (line 336)
4. ____ ablative	d. *regina* (line 334)
5. ____ accusative	e. *deseris* (line 323)
6. ____ dative	f. *praetendi* (line 339)
7. ____ genitive	g. *mei* (line 336)
8. ____ infinitive	h. *abscondere* (line 337)
9. ____ nominative	i. *cui* (line 323)
10. ____ vocative	j. *odere* (line 321)

Matching from lines 340–61

1. ____ *iussere* (line 346)	a. nominative plural
2. ____ *capessere* (line 346)	b. genitive plural
3. ____ *incendere* (line 360)	c. accusative plural
4. ____ *tecta* (line 343)	d. first person singular
5. ____ *mandata* (line 357)	e. nominative singular
6. ____ *divum* (line 356)	f. complementary infinitive
7. ____ *utrumque* (line 357)	g. third person plural
8. ____ *posuissem* (line 344)	h. accusative singular
9. ____ *imago* (line 353)	i. objective infinitive
10. ____ *Anchisae* (line 351)	j. genitive singular

Essay *Suggested time: 30 minutes*

There is a contrast between Dido's speech in lines 305–30 and Aeneas' speech in lines 333–61, both in tone and content. Which one is more effective, and why? Present your response in a well-organized essay using specific examples from throughout both speeches to support the points you make.

Support your assertions with references drawn from **throughout** the two passages (lines 305–30 and 333–61). All Latin words must be copied or their line numbers provided, AND they must be translated or paraphrased closely enough so that it is clear you understand the Latin. It is your responsibility to convince your reader that you are basing your conclusions on the Latin text and not merely on a general recollection of the passage. Direct your answer to the question; do not merely summarize the passage. Please write your essay on a separate piece of paper.

Scansion

Scan the following lines.

quin etiam hiberno moliri sidere classem

et mediis properas Aquilonibus ire per altum,

crudelis? quid, si non arva aliena domosque

(lines 309–11)

LESSON 23: BOOK IV. 362–449

Talia dicentem iamdudum aversa tuetur
huc illuc volvens oculos totumque pererrat
luminibus tacitis et sic accensa profatur:
"Nec tibi diva parens generis nec Dardanus auctor,
perfide, sed duris genuit te cautibus horrens
Caucasus Hyrcanaeque admorunt ubera tigres.
Nam quid dissimulo aut quae me ad maiora reservo?
Num fletu ingemuit nostro? Num lumina flexit?
Num lacrimas victus dedit aut miseratus amantem est?
Quae quibus anteferam? Iam iam nec maxima Iuno
nec Saturnius haec oculis pater aspicit aequis.
Nusquam tuta fides. Eiectum litore, egentem
excepi et regni demens in parte locavi.
Amissam classem, socios a morte reduxi
(heu furiis incensa feror!): nunc augur Apollo,
nunc Lyciae sortes, nunc et Iove missus ab ipso
interpres divum fert horrida iussa per auras.
Scilicet is superis labor est, ea cura quietos
sollicitat. Neque te teneo neque dicta refello:
i, sequere Italiam ventis, pete regna per undas.
Spero equidem mediis, si quid pia numina possunt,
supplicia hausurum scopulis et nomine Dido
saepe vocaturum. Sequar atris ignibus absens
et, cum frigida mors anima seduxerit artus,
omnibus umbra locis adero. Dabis, improbe, poenas.
Audiam et haec Manes veniet mihi fama sub imos."
His medium dictis sermonem abrumpit et auras
aegra fugit seque ex oculis avertit et aufert,
linquens multa metu cunctantem et multa parantem
dicere. Suscipiunt famulae conlapsaque membra
marmoreo referunt thalamo stratisque reponunt.

At pius Aeneas, quamquam lenire dolentem
solando cupit et dictis avertere curas,
multa gemens magnoque animum labefactus amore
iussa tamen divum exsequitur classemque revisit.
Tum vero Teucri incumbunt et litore celsas
deducunt toto naves. Natat uncta carina,
frondentesque ferunt remos et robora silvis
infabricata fugae studio.
Migrantes cernas totaque ex urbe ruentes:
ac velut ingentem formicae farris acervum
cum populant hiemis memores tectoque reponunt,

it nigrum campis agmen praedamque per herbas
convectant calle angusto: pars grandia trudunt
obnixae frumenta umeris, pars agmina cogunt
castigantque moras, opere omnis semita fervet.
Quis tibi tum, Dido, cernenti talia sensus,
quosve dabas gemitus, cum litora fervere late
prospiceres arce ex summa, totumque videres
misceri ante oculos tantis clamoribus aequor!
Improbe Amor, quid non mortalia pectora cogis!
Ire iterum in lacrimas, iterum temptare precando
cogitur et supplex animos summittere amori,
ne quid inexpertum frustra moritura relinquat.
"Anna, vides toto properari litore circum:
undique convenere; vocat iam carbasus auras,
puppibus et laeti nautae imposuere coronas.
Hunc ego si potui tantum sperare dolorem,
et perferre, soror, potero. Miserae hoc tamen unum
exsequere, Anna, mihi; solam nam perfidus ille
te colere, arcanos etiam tibi credere sensus;
sola viri molles aditus et tempora noras.
I, soror, atque hostem supplex adfare superbum:
non ego cum Danais Troianam exscindere gentem
Aulide iuravi classemve ad Pergama misi,
nec patris Anchisae cinerem manesve revelli:
cur mea dicta negat duras demittere in aures?
Quo ruit? Extremum hoc miserae det munus amanti:
exspectet facilemque fugam ventosque ferentes.
Non iam coniugium antiquum, quod prodidit, oro,
nec pulchro ut Latio careat regnumque relinquat:
tempus inane peto, requiem spatiumque furori,
dum mea me victam doceat fortuna dolere.
Extremam hanc oro veniam (miserere sororis),
quam mihi cum dederit cumulatam morte remittam."
Talibus orabat, talesque miserrima fletus
fertque refertque soror. Sed nullis ille movetur
fletibus aut voces ullas tractabilis audit;
fata obstant placidasque viri deus obstruit aures.
Ac velut annoso validam cum robore quercum
Alpini Boreae nunc hinc nunc flatibus illinc
eruere inter se certant; it stridor, et altae
consternunt terram concusso stipite frondes;
ipsa haeret scopulis et quantum vertice ad auras
aetherias, tantum radice in Tartara tendit:
haud secus adsiduis hinc atque hinc vocibus heros
tunditur, et magno persentit pectore curas;
mens immota manet, lacrimae volvuntur inanes.

Comprehension Questions

Translate and cite the line numbers of any Latin words or phrases that you use to support your answers.

1. Vergil here continues to use the imagery of fire, which he introduced at the beginning of Book 4 with the flames of love. With what words does he do this in lines 362–78, and how has the meaning of this image changed?

2. In lines 365–70, Vergil makes us sympathize with Dido's feeling that Aeneas is hard-hearted. How does Dido express this?

3. Dido expresses her feelings of betrayal in lines 373–76. With what phrases does she do this?

4. What threat does Dido make?

5. Vergil again shows that Aeneas is feeling torn in lines 393–96. With what phrases does he do this?

6. How does Vergil depict the Trojans' haste to depart?

7. How does Vergil make us sympathize with Dido in lines 408–12?

8. According to her speech to Anna, why does Dido find it so hard to bear Aeneas' departure?

9. What does Dido want Anna to request of Aeneas?

10. How does the simile in lines 441–48 contribute to our understanding of Aeneas' character?

11. To whom the tears of line 449 belong is ambiguous. Whose do you think they are? Why?

____

____

____

Short Answer Questions

Complete the statement or answer the question as appropriate.

1. *dicentem* (line 362) modifies the understood noun iadudum
2. *oculos* (line 363) is the object of pererrat
3. *accensa* (line 364) modifies the understood noun luminibus
4. The case of *perfide* (line 366) is ablative
5. *horrens* (line 366) modifies/describes ubera tigres
6. The tense of *admorunt* (line 367) is 3/pl [illegible]/ind.
7. *quid* (line 368) is translated what
8. *num* (line 370) introduces a question expecting the answer no
9. Lines 369–70 contain the rhetorical device hendiadys
10. *victus* (line 370) modifies the understood noun miseratus
11. The case of *quibus* (line 371) is ______
12. *nusquam tuta fides* (line 373) is translated ______
13. *eiectum* and *egentem* (line 373) modify the understood noun ______
14. *incensa* (line 376) modifies the understood pronoun ______
15. From lines 376–78 (*nunc . . . auras*), we learn that Dido believes/doesn't believe Aeneas. ______
16. Lines 376–78 contain the rhetorical device ______
17. The tone of lines 379–80 (*scilicet . . . sollicitat*) is ______
18. The case of *Dido* (line 383) is ______
19. The understood subject of *hausurum [esse]* (line 383) and *vocaturum [esse]* (line 384) is ______
20. *absens* (line 384) modifies the understood pronoun ______
21. The tense and mood of *seduxerit* (line 385) are ______
22. Copy out four verbs in the future tense from lines 386–87 ______

23. *se* (line 389) refers to ______________________________

24. *cunctantem* and *parantem* (line 390) modify the understood noun ______________________________

25. The form of *solando* (line 394) is ______________________________

26. *toto* (line 398) modifies/describes ______________________________

27. The simile (lines 402–407) compares ___ants___ to ___people___

28. The subject of *reponunt* (line 403) is ______________________________

29. The subject of *fervere* (line 409) is ______________________________

30. Line 412 contains the rhetorical device ______________________________

31. The form of *precando* (line 413) is ______________________________

32. In line 415, *relinquat* is subjunctive in what type of clause? ______________________________

33. In line 418, *laeti* modifies ______________________________

34. The infinitives *colere* and *credere* (line 422) are used ______________________________

35. The tense of *noras* (line 423) is ______________________________

36. In line 426, *–ve* connects ______________ and ______________

37. In line 427, *–ve* connects ______________ and ______________

38. The subject of *det* (line 429) is ______________________________

39. Who is the *miserae amanti* (line 429)? ______________________________

40. In line 432, *Latio* is ablative because ______________________________

41. In line 433, *inane* modifies ______________________________

42. In line 434, *dum* is translated ______________________________

43. The form of *miserere* (line 435) is ______________________________

44. The case of *fletus* (line 437) is ______________________________

45. The subject of *movetur* (line 438) is ______________________________

46. The simile (lines 441–49) compares ___tree___ to ___north winds___

47. *validam* (line 441) modifies ______________________________

48. *ipsa* (line 445) refers to ______________________________

49. *quantum* (line 445) is correlative with ______________________________

50. *heros* (line 447) refers to ______________________________

Translation *Suggested time: 20 minutes*

Translate the following passage as literally as possible.

Ac velut annoso validam cum robore quercum
Alpini Boreae nunc hinc nunc flatibus illinc
eruere inter se certant; it stridor, et altae
consternunt terram concusso stipite frondes;
ipsa haeret scopulis et quantum vertice ad auras
aetherias, tantum radice in Tartara tendit:
haud secus adsiduis hinc atque hinc vocibus heros
tunditur, et magno persentit pectore curas;

____

____

____

____

____

____

____

____

____

Short Answer Questions

Which item does not belong? Explain your reason.

1.	*iamdudum* (line 362)	*nusquam* (line 373)	*ac* (line 402)	*quo* (line 429)
2.	*exsequere* (line 421)	*credere* (line 422)	*i* (line 424)	*sequere* (line 381)
3.	*heros* (line 447)	*voces* (line 439)	*moras* (line 407)	*sermonem* (line 388)
4.	*Danais* (line 425)	*Dido* (line 408)	*Anna* (line 416)	*Amor* (line 412)
5.	*divum* (line 378)	*farris* (line 402)	*sororis* (line 435)	*miserae* (line 420)

1. Reason:__________________________________

2. Reason:__________________________________

3. Reason:__________________________________

4. Reason:____

5. Reason:____

What does each *–que* connect?

1. Line 392: __________________ and __________________
2. Line 395: __________________ and __________________
3. Line 396: __________________ and __________________
4. Line 399: __________________ and __________________
5. Line 401: __________________ and __________________
6. Line 403: __________________ and __________________
7. Line 404: __________________ and __________________
8. Line 407: __________________ and __________________
9. Line 410: __________________ and __________________

Essay *Suggested time: 30 minutes*

The complexity of Aeneas' character is seen in the description of him in lines 393–96 and in the simile in lines 441–49. What does Vergil want the reader to think of Aeneas based on these two passages? Do we sympathize with him? Using language from these two passages only, describe Aeneas' character in a well-organized essay.

Support your assertions with references drawn from **throughout** both passages. All Latin words must be copied or their line numbers provided, AND they must be translated or paraphrased closely enough so that it is clear you understand the Latin. It is your responsibility to convince your reader that you are basing your conclusions on the Latin text and not merely on a general recollection of the passages. Direct your answer to the question; do not merely summarize the passages. Please write your essay on a separate piece of paper.

Scansion

Scan the following lines.

misceri ante oculos tantis clamoribus aequor!
Improbe Amor, quid non mortalia pectora cogis!
Ire iterum in lacrimas, iterum temptare precando
cogitur et supplex animos summittere amori,

(lines 411–414)

Notes

LESSON 24: BOOK IV. 642–705

At trepida et coeptis immanibus effera Dido
sanguineam volvens aciem, maculisque trementes
interfusa genas et pallida morte futura,
interiora domus inrumpit limina et altos
conscendit furibunda rogos ensemque recludit
Dardanium, non hos quaesitum munus in usus.
Hic, postquam Iliacas vestes notumque cubile
conspexit, paulum lacrimis et mente morata
incubuitque toro dixitque novissima verba:
"Dulces exuviae, dum fata deusque sinebat,
accipite hanc animam meque his exsolvite curis.
Vixi et quem dederat cursum Fortuna peregi,
et nunc magna mei sub terras ibit imago.
Urbem praeclaram statui, mea moenia vidi,
ulta virum poenas inimico a fratre recepi,
felix, heu nimium felix, si litora tantum
numquam Dardaniae tetigissent nostra carinae."
Dixit, et os impressa toro "Moriemur inultae,
sed moriamur" ait. "Sic, sic iuvat ire sub umbras.
Hauriat hunc oculis ignem crudelis ab alto
Dardanus, et nostrae secum ferat omina mortis."
Dixerat, atque illam media inter talia ferro
conlapsam aspiciunt comites, ensemque cruore
spumantem sparsasque manus. It clamor ad alta
atria: concussam bacchatur Fama per urbem.
Lamentis gemituque et femineo ululatu
tecta fremunt, resonat magnis plangoribus aether,
non aliter quam si immissis ruat hostibus omnis
Karthago aut antiqua Tyros, flammaeque furentes
culmina perque hominum volvantur perque deorum.
Audiit exanimis trepidoque exterrita cursu
unguibus ora soror foedans et pectora pugnis
per medios ruit, ac morientem nomine clamat:
"Hoc illud, germana, fuit? Me fraude petebas?
Hoc rogus iste mihi, hoc ignes araeque parabant?
Quid primum deserta querar? Comitemne sororem
sprevisti moriens? Eadem me ad fata vocasses:
idem ambas ferro dolor atque eadem hora tulisset.
His etiam struxi manibus patriosque vocavi
voce deos, sic te ut posita, crudelis, abessem?
Exstinxti te meque, soror, populumque patresque
Sidonios urbemque tuam. Date, vulnera lymphis

abluam et, extremus si quis super halitus errat,
ore legam." Sic fata gradus evaserat altos,
semianimemque sinu germanam amplexa fovebat
cum gemitu atque atros siccabat veste cruores.
Illa graves oculos conata attollere rursus
deficit; infixum stridit sub pectore vulnus.
Ter sese attollens cubitoque adnixa levavit,
ter revoluta toro est oculisque errantibus alto
quaesivit caelo lucem ingemuitque reperta.
Tum Iuno omnipotens longum miserata dolorem
difficilesque obitus Irim demisit Olympo
quae luctantem animam nexosque resolveret artus.
Nam quia nec fato merita nec morte peribat,
sed misera ante diem subitoque accensa furore,
nondum illi flavum Proserpina vertice crinem
abstulerat Stygioque caput damnaverat Orco.
Ergo Iris croceis per caelum roscida pennis
mille trahens varios adverso sole colores
deuolat et supra caput astitit. "Hunc ego Diti
sacrum iussa fero teque isto corpore solvo":
sic ait et dextra crinem secat, omnis et una
dilapsus calor atque in ventos vita recessit.

Comprehension Questions

1. In lines 642–47, what physical symptoms show Dido's emotional state? ______________________

____

____

2. What two accomplishments of her own does Dido mention in her speech in lines 651–58?

____

____

____

3. Why is the use of the pluperfect subjunctive *tetigisset* (line 658) important? ______________

____

4. What words are contrasted in lines 656 and 659? What is the effect of this contrast?

____

____

____

5. Vergil used the word *ululante* in Book II.488 and uses *ululatu* in line 667. How do lines 667–71 recall the action of the scene in Book II? ______________________________

6. Anna expresses different emotions in her speech in lines 675–85. What are two of them? Support your answer with words or phrases from her speech and provide line references in parentheses.

7. How does Vergil show that Dido's death is slow and painful? ______________________________

8. Where else has Vergil depicted someone doing something "thrice," also repeating the word *ter* in the initial position of two successive lines? ______________________________

9. Why does Juno send Iris to Dido? ______________________________

10. Why, do you think, does Vergil stop, at this point in the poem, to give a description of Iris, the rainbow? ______________________________

Multiple Choice Questions *Suggested time: 20 minutes*

1. *aciem* in line 643 means
   a. eye
   b. sword

2. In line 644, *genas* is
   a. accusative of respect
   b. accusative direct object

3. *munus* (line 647) is in apposition to
   a. ensem
   b. *quaesitum*

4. In line 649, *morata* modifies
   a. *mente*
   b. Dido

5. *novissima* (line 650) here means
   a. newest
   b. last

6. *vixi* (line 653) implies that Dido feels that
   a. she has won at last
   b. she considers her life over

7. *se* (line 662) refers to
   a. Aeneas
   b. Dido

8. *conlapsam* (line 664) indicates that Dido has
   a. stabbed herself
   b. slipped

9. *sparsas* (line 665) is translated
   a. sparse
   b. spattered

10. How many elisions are in line 667?
    a. one
    b. two

11. *ruat* (line 669) is in a
    a. future-less-vivid ("should/would") condition
    b. present contrary-to-fact condition

12. –*que* (line 672) connects
    a. *exanimis* and *trepido*
    b. *exanimis* and *exterrita*

13. *pectora* (line 673) is the object of
    a. *foedans*
    b. *ruit*

14. *eadem* (line 678) modifies
    a. *me*
    b. *fata*

15. The form *tulisset* (line 679) indicates that
    a. something happened before the action of the main verb
    b. something had been desired but not received

16. *exstinxti* (line 682) is
    a. first person
    b. second person

17. *quis* (line 684) is translated
    a. who
    b. any

18. *illa* (line 688) refers to
    a. Anna
    b. Dido

19. *–que* (line 690) connects
    a. *attollens* and *adnixa*
    b. *sese* and *cubito*

20. *–que* (line 694) connects
    a. *dolorem* and *obitus*
    b. *miserata* and *difficiles*

21. Line 693 contains an example of
    a. chiasmus
    b. synchysis

22. *resolveret* (line 695) is in a
    a. clause of characteristic
    b. purpose clause

23. *illi* (line 698) refers to
    a. Iris
    b. Dido

24. Line 701 contains an example of
    a. chiasmus
    b. synchysis

25. *iussa* (line 703) is
    a. accusative plural neuter
    b. nominative singular feminine

26. *una* (line 704) here is an
    a. adverb
    b. adjective

Translation *Suggested time: 20 minutes*

Translate the following passage as literally as possible.

"Dulces exuviae, dum fata deusque sinebat,
accipite hanc animam meque his exsolvite curis.
Vixi et quem dederat cursum Fortuna peregi,
et nunc magna mei sub terras ibit imago.
Urbem praeclaram statui, mea moenia vidi,
ulta virum poenas inimico a fratre recepi,
felix, heu nimium felix, si litora tantum
numquam Dardaniae tetigissent nostra carinae."

Essays *Suggested time: 40 minutes (20 minutes per essay)*

1. Book IV begins with the lines *At regina gravi iamdudum saucia cura/ vulnus alit venis et caeco carpitur igni.* What language from this last section of Book IV echoes the metaphors with which Vergil opened the book? How has the meaning of the imagery changed? Present your response in a well-organized essay.

2. The simile in lines 667–71 recalls several earlier scenes in the *Aeneid*. Identify two such scenes and describe their relationship to this one. How does this simile offer an ironic inversion/reversal of those earlier events? Present your response in a well-organized essay.

For each essay above, support your assertions with references drawn from **throughout** the passage indicated by each essay. All Latin words must be copied or their line numbers provided, AND they must be translated or paraphrased closely enough so that it is clear you understand the Latin. It is your responsibility to convince your reader that you are basing your conclusions on the Latin text and not merely on a general recollection of the passage. Direct your answer to the question; do not merely summarize the passage. Please write your essays on a separate piece of paper.

Scansion

Indicate whether each line is scanned correctly or not.

1. _____ āccĭpĭ|t(e) hānc ănĭ|mām mĕquĕ |hīs ēx|sōlvĭtĕ |cūrīs (line 652)

2. _____ lāmēn|tīs gĕmĭ|tūqu(e) ēt |fēmĭnĕ|ō ūlŭ|lātū (line 667)

3. _____ cūlmĭnă| pērqu(e) hŏmĭ|nūm vōl|vāntūr |pērquĕ dĕ|ōrŭm (line 671)

4. _____ sēmĭă|nīmĕmquĕ| sīnŭ gĕr|mān(am) am|plēxă fŏv|ēbāt (line 686)

5. _____ sēd mĭsĕr(a) |āntĕ dĭ|ēm sŭbĭt|ōqu(e) āc|cēnsă fŭ|rōrĕ (line 697)

Book IV Comprehensive Review Essay

In Book IV Vergil uses speeches to convey Dido's inner conflict. Briefly describe three speeches given by Dido in Book IV. How do they differ? How are they similar? What does each one tell us about Dido's emotional state? Present your response in a well-organized essay. Make sure to cite and translate Latin from throughout the speeches to support your answer. Please write your essay on a separate piece of paper.

THE *AENEID* BOOK VI SELECTIONS WITH EXERCISES

LESSON 25: BOOK VI. 1–97

Sic fatur lacrimans, classique immittit habenas
et tandem Euboicis Cumarum adlabitur oris.
Obvertunt pelago proras; tum dente tenaci
ancora fundabat naves et litora curvae
praetexunt puppes. Iuvenum manus emicat ardens
litus in Hesperium; quaerit pars semina flammae
abstrusa in venis silicis, pars densa ferarum
tecta rapit silvas inventaque flumina monstrat.
At pius Aeneas arces quibus altus Apollo
praesidet horrendaeque procul secreta Sibyllae,
antrum immane, petit, magnam cui mentem animumque
Delius inspirat vates aperitque futura.
Iam subeunt Triviae lucos atque aurea tecta.
    Daedalus, ut fama est, fugiens Minoia regna
praepetibus pennis ausus se credere caelo
insuetum per iter gelidas enavit ad Arctos,
Chalcidicaque levis tandem super astitit arce.
Redditus his primum terris tibi, Phoebe, sacravit
remigium alarum posuitque immania templa.
In foribus letum Androgeo; tum pendere poenas
Cecropidae iussi (miserum!) septena quotannis
corpora natorum; stat ductis sortibus urna.
Contra elata mari respondet Cnosia tellus:
hic crudelis amor tauri suppostaque furto
Pasiphae mixtumque genus prolesque biformis
Minotaurus inest, Veneris monimenta nefandae,
hic labor ille domus et inextricabilis error;
magnum reginae sed enim miseratus amorem
Daedalus ipse dolos tecti ambagesque resolvit,
caeca regens filo vestigia. Tu quoque magnam
partem opere in tanto, sineret dolor, Icare, haberes.
Bis conatus erat casus effingere in auro,
bis patriae cecidere manus. Quin protinus omnia
perlegerent oculis, ni iam praemissus Achates
adforet atque una Phoebi Triviaeque sacerdos,
Deiphobe Glauci, fatur quae talia regi:
"Non hoc ista sibi tempus spectacula poscit;
nunc grege de intacto septem mactare iuvencos
praestiterit, totidem lectas ex more bidentes."
Talibus adfata Aenean (nec sacra morantur
iussa viri) Teucros vocat alta in templa sacerdos.

Excisum Euboicae latus ingens rupis in antrum,
quo lati ducunt aditus centum, ostia centum,
unde ruunt totidem voces, responsa Sibyllae.
Ventum erat ad limen, cum virgo "Poscere fata
tempus" ait; "Deus ecce deus!" Cui talia fanti
ante fores subito non vultus, non color unus,
non comptae mansere comae; sed pectus anhelum,
et rabie fera corda tument, maiorque videri
nec mortale sonans, adflata est numine quando
iam propiore dei. "Cessas in vota precesque,
Tros" ait "Aenea? Cessas? Neque enim ante dehiscent
attonitae magna ora domus." Et talia fata
conticuit. Gelidus Teucris per dura cucurrit
ossa tremor, funditque preces rex pectore ab imo:
"Phoebe, graves Troiae semper miserate labores,
Dardana qui Paridis derexti tela manusque
corpus in Aeacidae, magnas obeuntia terras
tot maria intravi duce te penitusque repostas
Massylum gentes praetentaque Syrtibus arva:
iam tandem Italiae fugientis prendimus oras.
Hac Troiana tenus fuerit fortuna secuta;
vos quoque Pergameae iam fas est parcere genti,
dique deaeque omnes, quibus obstitit Ilium et ingens
gloria Dardaniae. Tuque, o sanctissima vates,
praescia venturi, da (non indebita posco
regna meis fatis) Latio considere Teucros
errantesque deos agitataque numina Troiae.
Tum Phoebo et Triviae solido de marmore templum
instituam festosque dies de nomine Phoebi.
Te quoque magna manent regnis penetralia nostris:
hic ego namque tuas sortes arcanaque fata
dicta meae genti ponam, lectosque sacrabo,
alma, viros. Foliis tantum ne carmina manda,
ne turbata volent rapidis ludibria ventis;
ipsa canas oro." Finem dedit ore loquendi.

At Phoebi nondum patiens immanis in antro
bacchatur vates, magnum si pectore possit
excussisse deum; tanto magis ille fatigat
os rabidum, fera corda domans, fingitque premendo.
Ostia iamque domus patuere ingentia centum
sponte sua vatisque ferunt responsa per auras:
"O tandem magnis pelagi defuncte periclis
(sed terrae graviora manent), in regna Lavini
Dardanidae venient (mitte hanc de pectore curam),
sed non et venisse volent. Bella, horrida bella,
et Thybrim multo spumantem sanguine cerno.

Non Simois tibi nec Xanthus nec Dorica castra
defuerint; alius Latio iam partus Achilles,
natus et ipse dea; nec Teucris addita Iuno
usquam aberit, cum tu supplex in rebus egenis
quas gentes Italum aut quas non oraveris urbes!
Causa mali tanti coniunx iterum hospita Teucris
externique iterum thalami.
Tu ne cede malis, sed contra audentior ito,
qua tua te Fortuna sinet. Via prima salutis
(quod minime reris) Graia pandetur ab urbe."

Comprehension Questions

Translate the Latin you use in your answers.

1. Why is Aeneas weeping at the beginning of Book VI? ______

2. Why is the Italian shore called *Euboicis* (line 2)? ______

3. Why, do you think, does Vergil, at this point in the narrative, insert Daedalus' story and the description of the temple he built? Are there any themes alluded to in lines 14–33 that appear elsewhere in the *Aeneid*?

4. Why does Vergil call Daedalus' journey *insuetum* (line 16)? ______

5. Who in Roman history erected a famous temple to Apollo? Where did he locate it? ______

6. From your knowledge of mythology, explain the reason the Athenians were ordered to pay penalties (lines 20–21). ______

7. Why is Venus called *nefandae* (line 26)? ______

8. With his mention of the thread that Daedalus uses to navigate the labyrinth, Vergil alludes to another version of the myth of the Minotaur involving Minos' daughter. What is this story? What happens to Minos' daughter? ______

9. From your knowledge of mythology, explain what happened to Icarus. ______

10. In lines 62–65, what does Aeneas request of Apollo? ______

11. In lines 69–74, what does Aeneas say he will do in return for requests granted by Apollo and the Sibyl?

______

12. What might have happened if Aeneas had not made the request he does in lines 74–76?

____

____

13. What does Deiphobe predict will happen to the Trojans when they reach their destination? How do you think this makes Aeneas and his men feel? _______________

____

____

____

14. What is the Greek city in line 97 of which Deiphobe speaks? _______________

____

____

____

Multiple Choice Questions *Suggested time: 55 minutes*

1. To which word is *silvas* (line 8) in apposition?
   a. *densa* (line 7)
   b. *tecta* (line 8)
   c. *inventa* (line 8)
   d. *flumina* (line 8)

2. The conjunction *–que* (line 10) connects
   a. *arces* and *secreta*
   b. *Apollo* and *Sibyllae*
   c. *praesidet* and *petit*
   d. *altus* and *procul*

3. To which word is *antrum* (line 11) in apposition?
   a. *arces* (line 9)
   b. *Apollo* (line 9)
   c. *secreta* (line 10)
   d. *animum* (line 11)

4. *Minoia regna* (line 14) is
   a. Euboea
   b. Greece
   c. Crete
   d. Phoenicia

5. In line 16, *gelidas* modifies
   a. *pennis* (line 15)
   b. *iter* (line 16)
   c. *Arctos* (line 16)
   d. *levis* (line 17)

6. The adjective *Chalcidica* (line 17) is formed from the name of the city in
   a. Euboea
   b. Greece
   c. Crete
   d. Phoenicia

7. Line 20 begins a(n)
   a. simile
   b. metaphor
   c. ecphrasis
   d. pathetic fallacy

8. The case of *Androgeo* (line 20) is
   a. genitive
   b. dative
   c. accusative
   d. ablative

9. The *Cecropidae* (line 21) are
   a. Cretans
   b. Spartans
   c. Tyrians
   d. Athenians

10. To which word is *corpora* (line 22) in apposition?
   a. *poenas* (line 20)
   b. *Cecropidae* (line 21)
   c. *septena* (line 21)
   d. *urna* (line 22)

11. In line 23, *elata* modifies
   a. *urna* (line 22)
   b. *contra* (line 23)
   c. *mari* (line 23)
   d. *tellus* (line 23)

12. The case of *Pasiphae* (line 25) is
   a. nominative
   b. genitive
   c. dative
   d. ablative

13. Line 26 contains an example of
   a. synchysis
   b. chiasmus
   c. anastrophe
   d. metonymy

14. In line 29, *ambages* is an allusion to
   a. Daedalus' wanderings
   b. the Trojan horse
   c. the maze
   d. the Minotaur

15. From lines 30–33 (*tu . . . manus*), we can infer that
   a. Daedalus did not have the skill to depict Icarus
   b. Icarus had too great a part in the work
   c. a band of men twice kept Daedalus from working in gold
   d. Daedalus was grieving too much to depict Icarus

16. The verb *sineret* (line 31) is in a(n)
    a. purpose clause
    b. present contrary-to-fact condition
    c. indirect statement
    d. indirect question

17. Line 31 contains an example of
    a. litotes
    b. hendiadys
    c. anastrophe
    d. apostrophe

18. The verb *adforet* (line 35) is in a(n)
    a. purpose clause
    b. present contrary-to-fact condition
    c. past contrary-to-fact condition
    d. indirect question

19. The phrase *ex more* in line 39 is best translated
    a. according to custom
    b. from delay
    c. out of habit
    d. out of manner

20. The word *adfata* In line 40 modifies
    a. *Aenean* (line 40)
    b. *sacra* (line 40)
    c. *Teucros* (line 41)
    d. *sacerdos* (line 41)

21. To which word is *responsa* (line 44) in apposition?
    a. *aditus* (line 43)
    b. *ostia* (line 43)
    c. *voces* (line 44)
    d. *Sibyllae* (line 44)

22. Deiphobe's appearance in lines 47–50 (*subito . . . sonans*) is the result of
    a. love
    b. illness
    c. inspiration
    d. confusion

23. According to the Sibyl's speech in lines 51–53 (*cessas . . . domus*), what must Aeneas do?
    a. pray
    b. enter the house
    c. stay longer
    d. let his mouth gape open

24. Line 53 contains an example of
    a. synecdoche
    b. chiasmus
    c. metonymy
    d. tmesis

25. From lines 54–55 (*gelidus . . . imo*), we can infer that
    a. the Trojans are frightened
    b. the Sibyl's cave is cold
    c. the Sibyl's words are harsh
    d. Aeneas knows that his words are precious

26. The form of *miserate* (line 56) is
    a. plural imperative
    b. an adverb
    c. ablative noun
    d. vocative participle

27. The verb *derexti* (line 57) is
    a. first person perfect
    b. second person perfect
    c. passive infinitive
    d. perfect participle

28. *Aeacidae* (line 58) is another name for
    a. Turnus
    b. Diomedes
    c. Achilles
    d. Sarpedon

29. The ablative use of *duce* (line 59) is
    a. means
    b. separation
    c. agent
    d. absolute

30. Line 62 contains an example of
    a. tmesis
    b. chiasmus
    c. enallage
    d. hyperbaton

31. *Troiana fuerit fortuna secuta* (line 62) is best translated
    a. Trojan fortune will have followed
    b. let Trojan fortune have followed
    c. Trojan fortune may follow
    d. if only Trojan fortune had followed

32. Line 66 contains an example of
    a. litotes
    b. zeugma
    c. tmesis
    d. prolepsis

33. *Latio* in line 67 is best translated
    a. from Latium
    b. by Latium
    c. with Latium
    d. in Latium

34. In lines 69–70 (*tum . . . Phoebi*) Vergil is
    a. showing why the Romans worshipped Hecate
    b. foretelling the Roman expertise at building
    c. explaining Augustus' lineage
    d. making an allusion to institutions revived by Augustus

35. In line 72, Vergil makes an allusion to
    a. the Sibylline books
    b. the Twelve Tables
    c. choosing priests by lot
    d. the Vestal Virgins

36. In lines 74–76 (*foliis . . . oro*), Aeneas makes a request he was advised to in Book III by

a. Anchises
b. Helenus
c. Celaeno
d. Andromache

37. The form of *canas* (line 76) is

a. accusative plural noun
b. nominative singular noun
c. present indicative verb
d. present subjunctive verb

38. The antecedent for *sua* in line 82 is

a. *ostia* (line 81)
b. *domus* (line 81)
c. *ingentia* (line 81)
d. *vatis* (line 82)

39. The form of *defuncte* (line 83) is

a. imperative verb
b. ablative noun
c. vocative participle
d. vocative noun

40. The case of *periclis* (line 83) is

a. genitive
b. dative
c. accusative
d. ablative

41. In lines 88–89 (*non . . . defuerint*), the Sibyl implies that

a. the Aeneadae will have to fight the equivalent of another Trojan war
b. the terrain of Rome will be similar to that of Troy
c. the Greeks will be awaiting the Aeneadae in Italy
d. although they failed in the Trojan war, the Aeneadae will succeed in Italy

42. Although Aeneas does not know it, *alius Achilles* (line 89) will be

a. Evander
b. Latinus
c. Turnus
d. Euryalus

43. In lines 91–92 (*cum . . . urbes*), the Sibyl predicts that

a. Aeneas will eventually rule over many peoples
b. the Italians will have to come to Aeneas in supplication
c. the towns of Italy will someday worship Aeneas
d. Aeneas will have to ask for help from many people

44. Although Aeneas does not know it, the *coniunx* (line 93) will be

a. Lavinia
b. Amata
c. Andromache
d. Camilla

45. Lines 93–94 contain an example of
  a. litotes
  b. hiatus
  c. anaphora
  d. metaphor

46. The form of *ito* (line 95) is
  a. future indicative
  b. present indicative
  c. ablative participle
  d. imperative

47. The Sibyl says *quod minime reris* (line 97) because
  a. the Trojans will have to fight the Greeks again
  b. Greeks will help Aeneas
  c. the Trojans will have to go to another Greek city
  d. the Trojans will have to make their way from a Greek city

Translation *Suggested time: 15 minutes*

Translate the following passage as literally as possible.

At Phoebi nondum patiens immanis in antro
bacchatur vates, magnum si pectore possit
excussisse deum; tanto magis ille fatigat
os rabidum, fera corda domans, fingitque premendo.
Ostia iamque domus patuere ingentia centum
sponte sua vatisque ferunt responsa per auras:

____

____

____

____

____

____

____

Short Answer Questions

Matching

1.	____ Cumae	a.	city on Crete
2.	____ Euboea	b.	river near Troy
3.	____ Delos	c.	island where Minos was once king
4.	____ Chalchis	d.	island where Apollo was born
5.	____ Cnossos	e.	river that runs through Rome
6.	____ Crete	f.	a town in southern Italy
7.	____ Syrtis	g.	area of central Italy
8.	____ Thybris	h.	shallows/quicksand off the coast of north Africa
9.	____ Simois	i.	island off the eastern coast of Greece; origin of the colonists of Cumae
10.	____ Latium	j.	city in Euboea

Essay *Suggested time: 20 minutes*

In a well-organized essay, discuss how the ecphrasis in lines 14–33 reflects themes encountered earlier in the *Aeneid*.

Support your assertions with references drawn from **these lines**. All Latin words must be copied or their line numbers provided, AND they must be translated or paraphrased closely enough so that it is clear you understand the Latin. It is your responsibility to convince your reader that you are basing your conclusions on the Latin text and not merely on a general recollection of the passage. Direct your answer to the question; do not merely summarize the passage. Please write your essay on a separate piece of paper.

Scansion

Scan the following lines.

et tandem Euboicis Cumarum adlabitur oris (line 2)

remigium alarum posuitque immania templa (line 19)

iussa viri, Teucros vocat alta in templa sacerdos (line 41)

causa mali tanti coniunx iterum hospita Teucris (line 93)

LESSON 26: BOOK VI. 98–211

Talibus ex adyto dictis Cumaea Sibylla
horrendas canit ambages antroque remugit,
obscuris uera inuoluens: ea frena furenti
concutit et stimulos sub pectore uertit Apollo.
Ut primum cessit furor et rabida ora quierunt,
incipit Aeneas heros: "Non ulla laborum,
o virgo, noua mi facies inopinave surgit;
omnia praecepi atque animo mecum ante peregi.
Unum oro: quando hic inferni ianua regis
dicitur et tenebrosa palus Acheronte refuso,
ire ad conspectum cari genitoris et ora
contingat; doceas iter et sacra ostia pandas.
Illum ego per flammas et mille sequentia tela
eripui his umeris medioque ex hoste recepi;
ille meum comitatus iter maria omnia mecum
atque omnis pelagique minas caelique ferebat,
invalidus, vires ultra sortemque senectae.
Quin, ut te supplex peterem et tua limina adirem,
idem orans mandata dabat. Gnatique patrisque,
alma, precor, miserere (potes namque omnia, nec te
nequiquam lucis Hecate praefecit Avernis),
si potuit manes accersere coniugis Orpheus
Threicia fretus cithara fidibusque canoris,
si fratrem Pollux alterna morte redemit
itque reditque viam totiens. Quid Thesea, magnum
quid memorem Alciden? Et mi genus ab Iove summo."
Talibus orabat dictis arasque tenebat,
cum sic orsa loqui vates: "Sate sanguine divum,
Tros Anchisiade, facilis descensus Averno:
noctes atque dies patet atri ianua Ditis;
sed revocare gradum superasque evadere ad auras,
hoc opus, hic labor est. Pauci, quos aequus amavit
Iuppiter aut ardens evexit ad aethera virtus,
dis geniti potuere. Tenent media omnia silvae,
Cocytusque sinu labens circumvenit atro.
Quod si tantus amor menti, si tanta cupido est
bis Stygios innare lacus, bis nigra videre
Tartara, et insano iuvat indulgere labori,
accipe quae peragenda prius. Latet arbore opaca
aureus et foliis et lento vimine ramus,
Iunoni infernae dictus sacer; hunc tegit omnis
lucus et obscuris claudunt convallibus umbrae.

Sed non ante datur telluris operta subire
auricomos quam quis decerpserit arbore fetus.
Hoc sibi pulchra suum ferri Proserpina munus
instituit. Primo avulso non deficit alter
aureus, et simili frondescit virga metallo.
Ergo alte vestiga oculis et rite repertum
carpe manu; namque ipse volens facilisque sequetur,
si te fata vocant; aliter non viribus ullis
vincere nec duro poteris convellere ferro.
Praeterea iacet exanimum tibi corpus amici
(heu nescis) totamque incestat funere classem,
dum consulta petis nostroque in limine pendes.
Sedibus hunc refer ante suis et conde sepulcro.
Duc nigras pecudes; ea prima piacula sunto.
Sic demum lucos Stygis et regna invia vivis
aspicies." Dixit, pressoque obmutuit ore.
    Aeneas maesto defixus lumina vultu
ingreditur linquens antrum, caecosque volutat
eventus animo secum. Cui fidus Achates
it comes et paribus curis vestigia figit.
Multa inter sese vario sermone serebant,
quem socium exanimum vates, quod corpus humandum
diceret. Atque illi Misenum in litore sicco,
ut venere, vident indigna morte peremptum,
Misenum Aeoliden, quo non praestantior alter
aere ciere viros Martemque accendere cantu.
Hectoris hic magni fuerat comes, Hectora circum
et lituo pugnas insignis obibat et hasta.
Postquam illum vita victor spoliavit Achilles,
Dardanio Aeneae sese fortissimus heros
addiderat socium, non inferiora secutus.
Sed tum, forte cava dum personat aequora concha,
demens, et cantu vocat in certamina divos,
aemulus exceptum Triton, si credere dignum est,
inter saxa virum spumosa immerserat unda.
Ergo omnes magno circum clamore fremebant,
praecipue pius Aeneas. Tum iussa Sibyllae,
haud mora, festinant flentes aramque sepulcri
congerere arboribus caeloque educere certant.
Itur in antiquam silvam, stabula alta ferarum;
procumbunt piceae, sonat icta securibus ilex
fraxineaeque trabes cuneis et fissile robur
scinditur, advolvunt ingentis montibus ornos.
    Nec non Aeneas opera inter talia primus
hortatur socios paribusque accingitur armis.
Atque haec ipse suo tristi cum corde volutat
aspectans silvam immensam, et sic forte precatur:

"Si nunc se nobis ille aureus arbore ramus
ostendat nemore in tanto! Quando omnia vere
heu nimium de te vates, Misene, locuta est."
Vix ea fatus erat, geminae cum forte columbae
ipsa sub ora viri caelo venere volantes,
et viridi sedere solo. Tum maximus heros
maternas agnovit aves laetusque precatur:
"Este duces, o, si qua via est, cursumque per auras
derigite in lucos ubi pinguem dives opacat
ramus humum. Tuque, o, dubiis ne defice rebus,
diva parens." Sic effatus vestigia pressit
observans quae signa ferant, quo tendere pergant.
Pascentes illae tantum prodire volando
quantum acie possent oculi servare sequentum.
Inde ubi venere ad fauces grave olentis Averni,
tollunt se celeres liquidumque per aëra lapsae
sedibus optatis gemina super arbore sidunt,
discolor unde auri per ramos aura refulsit.
Quale solet silvis brumali frigore viscum
fronde virere nova, quod non sua seminat arbos,
et croceo fetu teretes circumdare truncos,
talis erat species auri frondentis opaca
ilice, sic leni crepitabat brattea vento.
Corripit Aeneas extemplo avidusque refringit
cunctantem, et vatis portat sub tecta Sibyllae.

Comprehension Questions

Where appropriate, support your answers with words or phrases from the Latin, translate them, and cite the line numbers.

1. Has the prophetess told Aeneas anything he had not already known?________________________

____

2. Aeneas gives an eloquent and moving summary of his relationship with his father in lines 108–17. What does he say that gives us a clear understanding of how he feels about his father?

____

____

____

____

____

3. From your knowledge of mythology, explain briefly the tales of Orpheus, Pollux, Theseus, and Hercules, and why it is relevant that Aeneas mentions them in lines 119–23.

4. In line 126, the Sibyl says that the trip to the underworld is easy. What then is difficult, according to her? Why does she use the word *bis* in regard to the journey (lines 126–35)?

5. Why is the golden bough so important?

6. Why was Misenus killed?

7. How does Venus help, indirectly, Aeneas in his search for the golden bough? ________________

8. How does the simile in lines 205–7 help describe the golden bough? ________________

9. Why, do you think, does Vergil describe the bough as *cunctantem* (line 211)? ________________

Multiple Choice Questions *Suggested time: 25 minutes*

Choose the better translation.

1. *obscuris vera involvens* (line 100)
   a. [she], true, wrapping in obscure matters
   b. [she] wrapping truth in obscurity

2. *ire ad conspectum cari genitoris et ora/ contingat* (lines 108–9)
   a. may it befall me to go to the view and face of my dear father
   b. would that it befall me to go to the view of my dear father and to his shores

3. *gnatique patrisque/ alma, precor, miserere (potes namque omnia, nec te/ nequiquam lucis Hecate praefecit Avernis)* (lines 116–18)
   a. pity both a son and a father, kind one, I entreat you (for you are able to do all things, nor in vain did Hecate put you in charge of the groves of Avernus)
   b. I entreat you, kind one, [since] you are able to pity both a father and a son (for you are able to do all things, nor in vain did Hecate set you over the grove near Avernus)

4. *pauci, quos aequus amavit/ Iuppiter aut ardens evexit ad aethera virtus,/ dis geniti potuere* (lines 129–31)
   a. few, having been born, whom impartial Jupiter loved or bore to the burning heavens, were able [to show] courage to the gods
   b. few, having been born from gods, whom impartial Jupiter loved or burning courage carried to the heavens, have been able

5. *accipe quae peragenda prius* (line 136)
   a. you, first, learn what things had to be accomplished
   b. learn what things must be accomplished first

6. *sed non ante datur telluris operta subire/ auricomos quam quis decerpserit arbore fetus* (lines 140–41)
   a. but it is not granted to enter the hidden part of earth before someone will have plucked the golden-leaved growth from the tree
   b. but not before is it granted to enter the earth's hidden part until which [time] someone has plucked the golden-leaved growth from the tree

7. *primo avulso non deficit alter/ aureus, et simili frondescit virga metallo* (lines 143–44)
   a. at first, with it torn off, another golden one is not lacking, and it sprouts a [new] branch with a similar metal
   b. with the first torn off, a second golden one is not lacking, and the branch sprouts with a similar metal

8. *namque ipse volens facilisque sequetur,/ si te fata vocant* (lines 146–47)
   a. for it itself willing and easy would follow, if the fates should call you
   b. for it itself willing and easy will follow, if the fates call you

9. *sic demum lucos Stygis et regna invia vivis/ aspicies* (lines 154–55)
   a. thus at last you should see the groves of Styx and the realms unlivable for the living
   b. thus at last you will see the groves of Styx and the realms pathless for the living

10. *multa inter sese vario sermone serebant/ quem socium exanimum vates, quod corpus humandum/ diceret* (lines 160–62)
   a. they were discussing many things between themselves in a diverse conversation, which lifeless comrade the priestess spoke of, which body had to be buried
   b. they were discussing many things among themselves in a diverse conversation, whom the priestess would say was their lifeless comrade, what she would say was the body that had to be buried

11. *quo non praestantior alter/ aere ciere viros Martemque accendere cantu* (lines 164–65)
   a. with which trumpet another not more excellent at being able to stir the men and with which song to kindle war
   b. than whom another was not more excellent in stirring up the men with his trumpet and kindling war with his song

12. *Dardanio Aeneae sese fortissimus heros/ addiderat socium, non inferiora secutus* (lines 169–70)
    a. the bravest hero had added himself as a comrade to Trojan Aeneas, having attended no lesser matters
    b. that bravest one had added himself as a comrade to the Trojan hero Aeneas, attending no lesser matters

13. *tum iussa Sibyllae,/ haud mora, festinant flentes aramque sepulcri/ congerere arboribus caeloque educere certant* (lines 176–78)
    a. then, weeping, they hurry [to complete] the orders of the Sibyl, there is no delay, and they strive to heap with branches an altar of a tomb and to raise it to the sky
    b. then, with the Sibyl's orders not having been delayed, they hurry, weeping, to gather branches for an altar of a tomb and to raise them to the sky

14. *sonat ictus securibus ilex/ fraxineaeque trabes cuneis et fissile robur/ scinditur* (lines 180–82)
    a. struck with sureness, the holm-oak resounds, and the timbers and the cleavable oak is split with wedges of ash
    b. struck with axes, the holm-oak resounds, and the ashen timber and cleavable oak is split with wedges

15. *si nunc se nobis ille aureus arbore ramus/ ostendat nemore in tanto! quando omnia vere/ heu nimium de te vates, Misene, locuta est* (lines 187–89)
    a. if now that golden branch should show itself to us on a tree in such a great grove! since truly the prophetess spoke so much, alas, about you, Misenus
    b. I wish that branch, golden on a tree, would show itself to us in such a great grove! since the prophetess spoke everything too truly, alas, about you, Misenus

16. *geminae cum forte columbae/ ipsa sub ora viri caelo venere volantes,/ et viridi sedere solo* (lines 190–92)
    a. when by chance two doves came flying from the sky before the very face of the man and settled on the fresh earth
    b. two doves came with courage before the very face of the man and wanting to settle on the fresh earth

17. *pascentes illae tantum prodire volando/ quantum acie possent oculi servare sequentum* (lines 199–200)
    a. they, enduring to advance so much by flying as much as they could observe by the line of sight of those following
    b. they, feeding, advance by flying only so far as the eyes of those following could observe with their eyesight

18. *tollunt se celeres liquidumque per aera lapsae/ sedibus optatis gemina super arbore sidunt* (lines 202–3)
    a. the two [birds] lift themselves, swift, and gliding through the clear air to their desired places, they settle on top of the tree
    b. they lift themselves, swift, and gliding through the liquid air they settle in their desired places on top of the twin tree

19. *quale solet silvis brumali frigore viscum/ fronde virere nova, quod non sua seminat arbos* (lines 205–6)
   a. such as the mistletoe, which its own tree does not produce, is accustomed to flourish with new foliage during the wintry frost in the woods
   b. such as chill-bearing mistletoe, because its own tree does not produce, is accustomed to flourish with new foliage during the winter in the woods

20. *talis erat species auri frondentis opaca/ ilice, sic leni crepitabat brattea vento* (lines 208–9)
   a. such was the appearance of the leafy gold in the shady holm-oak, thus the foil rustled in the gentle wind
   b. such was the appearance of the gold in the foliage of the shady holm-oak, thus the foil rustled gently in the wind

Translation *Suggested time: 15 minutes*

Translate the following passage as literally as possible.

Talibus orabat dictis arasque tenebat,
cum sic orsa loqui vates: "Sate sanguine divum,
Tros Anchisiade, facilis descensus Averno:
noctes atque dies patet atri ianua Ditis;
sed revocare gradum superasque evadere ad auras,
hoc opus, hic labor est.

Short Answer Questions

From lines 98–129, find, copy out, and provide line references in parentheses for:

1. an example of polyptoton ______
2. a deliberative subjunctive ______
3. a patronymic in the vocative ______
4. a line with three elisions ______
5. an imperative ______
6. an example of anastrophe ______
7. a participle in the vocative ______
8. an example of anaphora ______
9. an accusative of extent/duration of time ______
10. a patronymic in the accusative ______

From lines 130–55, find, copy out, and provide line references in parentheses for:

1. a passive infinitive ______
2. a verb in the future perfect ______
3. three verbs in the future ______
4. an example of anaphora ______
5. a third person imperative ______
6. an example of asyndeton ______
7. a present participle in the nominative, singular, feminine ______
8. an adverb that means "otherwise" ______
9. a passive periphrastic ______
10. an adverb that means "in addition" or "besides" ______

From lines 156–84, find, copy out, and provide line references in parentheses for:

1. an example of epanalepsis ______
2. an example of litotes ______
3. *ut* meaning "as" ______

4. a fourth declension noun in the accusative ______________________

5. two perfect passive participles in the accusative ______________________

6. a verb in the Greek middle ______________________

7. an example of polyptoton ______________________

8. a verb used impersonally ______________________

9. a patronymic ______________________

From lines 185–211, find, copy out, and provide line references in parentheses for:

1. a present participle in the accusative ______________________

2. four present participles in the nominative ______________________

   ____

3. a word introducing a simile ______________________

4. a relative clause ______________________

5. two indirect questions ______________________

6. an accusative object of a present participle ______________________

7. a fourth declension noun in the ablative ______________________

8. a gerund ______________________

9. a superlative ______________________

10. two complementary infinitives ______________________

Essay *Suggested time: 20 minutes*

Why has Vergil inserted the episode on the death and funeral of Misenus at this point in the narrative? What lesson about the relationship between humans and the gods does this episode provide? Present your response in a well-organized essay.

This essay does not require Latin citation. Your answer requires analysis; do not merely summarize the narrative. Please write your essay on a separate piece of paper.

Scansion

Scan the following lines.

ut venere, vident indigna morte peremptum,
Misenum Aeoliden, quo non praestantior alter
aere ciere viros Martemque accendere cantu.
Hectoris hic magni fuerat comes, Hectora circum

(lines 163–166)

Notes

LESSON 27A: BOOK VI. 450–476

Inter quas Phoenissa recens a vulnere Dido
errabat silva in magna; quam Troius heros
ut primum iuxta stetit agnovitque per umbras
obscuram, qualem primo qui surgere mense
aut videt aut vidisse putat per nubila lunam,
demisit lacrimas dulcique adfatus amore est:
"Infelix Dido, verus mihi nuntius ergo
venerat exstinctam ferroque extrema secutam?
Funeris heu tibi causa fui? Per sidera iuro,
per superos et si qua fides tellure sub ima est,
invitus, regina, tuo de litore cessi.
Sed me iussa deum, quae nunc has ire per umbras,
per loca senta situ cogunt noctemque profundam,
imperiis egere suis; nec credere quivi
hunc tantum tibi me discessu ferre dolorem.
Siste gradum teque aspectu ne subtrahe nostro.
Quem fugis? Extremum fato quod te adloquor hoc est."
Talibus Aeneas ardentem et torva tuentem
lenibat dictis animum lacrimasque ciebat.
Illa solo fixos oculos aversa tenebat
nec magis incepto vultum sermone movetur
quam si dura silex aut stet Marpesia cautes.
Tandem corripuit sese atque inimica refugit
in nemus umbriferum, coniunx ubi pristinus illi
respondet curis aequatque Sychaeus amorem.
Nec minus Aeneas casu percussus iniquo
prosequitur lacrimis longe et miseratur euntem.

Comprehension Questions

1. What literal wound (line 450) is Dido bearing? What figurative one? ______________________

____

____

____

2. From the simile in lines 453–54, how are we supposed to imagine Dido? How does this image differ from the one in the simile in Book I.498–502 with which Vergil introduced her to us?

3. What different feelings does Aeneas have in lines 458–66?

4. Line 469 is very similar to Book I.482. In both cases, what reaction is the subject showing?

5. Line 471 recalls Dido's description of Aeneas in Book IV.366–67. Why does Vergil make this implicit comparison?

6. Why is Aeneas crying in line 476?

Multiple Choice Questions *Suggested time: 12 minutes*

1. The best translation of *ut primum* (line 452) is
   a. in order that at first
   b. with the result that at first
   c. as soon as
   d. as at first

2. In line 453, *qualem* modifies
   a. *Dido* (line 450)
   b. *qui* (line 453)
   c. *mense* (line 453)
   d. *lunam* (line 454)

3. The best translation of *ferroque extrema secutam* (line 457) is
   a. [and that you] had sought your death with a sword
   b. [and that you] would see your death with a sword
   c. [and you] having followed the final things with a sword
   d. [and that you] in your death pursued it with a sword

4. In line 459, *qua* modifies
   a. *sidera* (line 458)
   b. *fides* (line 459)
   c. *tellure* (line 459)
   d. *ima* (line 459)

5. The antecedent of *quae* (line 461) is
   a. *me* (line 461)
   b. *iussa* (line 461)
   c. *deum* (line 461)
   d. *loca* (line 462)

6. The form of *discessu* (line 464) is
   a. supine
   b. ablative participle
   c. ablative noun
   d. adverb

7. In line 464, *ferre* is a(n)
   a. infinitive in indirect statement
   b. objective infinitive
   c. historical infinitive
   d. complementary infinitive

8. In line 468, *lenibat* is best translated
   a. was soothing
   b. used to soothe
   c. was trying to soothe
   d. began to soothe

9. The best translation of *solo* (line 469) is
   a. alone
   b. on the ground
   c. towards him alone
   d. from the ground

10. The Latin word *pristinus* (line 473) means
    a. former
    b. pristine
    c. untouched
    d. outstanding

Translation *Suggested time: 20 minutes*

Translate the following passage as literally as possible.

Illa solo fixos oculos aversa tenebat
nec magis incepto vultum sermone movetur
quam si dura silex aut stet Marpesia cautes.
Tandem corripuit sese atque inimica refugit
in nemus umbriferum, coniunx ubi pristinus illi
respondet curis aequatque Sychaeus amorem.
Nec minus Aeneas casu percussus iniquo
prosequitur lacrimis longe et miseratur euntem.

Essay

What emotions does Aeneas convey with his speech in lines 456–66? How effective is he? Provide your response in a well-organized essay.

Support your assertions with references drawn from **throughout** this passage (lines 456–66 only). All Latin words must be copied or their line numbers provided, AND they must be translated or paraphrased closely enough so that it is clear you understand the Latin. It is your responsibility to convince your reader that you are basing your conclusions on the Latin text and not merely on a general recollection of the passage. Direct your answer to the question; do not merely summarize the passage. Please write your essay on a separate piece of paper.

Scansion

Scan the following lines.

quam si dura silex aut stet Marpesia cautes.
tandem corripuit sese atque inimica refugit
in nemus umbriferum, coniunx ubi pristinus illi
respondet curis aequatque Sychaeus amorem.

(lines 471–74)

LESSON 27B: BOOK VI. 847–901

"Excudent alii spirantia mollius aera
(credo equidem), vivos ducent de marmore vultus,
orabunt causas melius, caelique meatus
describent radio et surgentia sidera dicent:
tu regere imperio populos, Romane, memento
(hae tibi erunt artes), pacique imponere morem,
parcere subiectis et debellare superbos."
Sic pater Anchises, atque haec mirantibus addit:
"Aspice, ut insignis spoliis Marcellus opimis
ingreditur victorque viros supereminet omnes.
Hic rem Romanam magno turbante tumultu
sistet eques, sternet Poenos Gallumque rebellem,
tertiaque arma patri suspendet capta Quirino."
Atque hic Aeneas (una namque ire videbat
egregium forma iuvenem et fulgentibus armis,
sed frons laeta parum et deiecto lumina vultu)
"Quis, pater, ille, virum qui sic comitatur euntem?
Filius, anne aliquis magna de stirpe nepotum?
Qui strepitus circa comitum! Quantum instar in ipso!
Sed nox atra caput tristi circumvolat umbra."
Tum pater Anchises lacrimis ingressus obortis:
"O gnate, ingentem luctum ne quaere tuorum;
ostendent terris hunc tantum fata nec ultra
esse sinent. Nimium vobis Romana propago
visa potens, superi, propria haec si dona fuissent.

Quantos ille virum magnam Mavortis ad urbem
campus aget gemitus! Vel quae, Tiberine, videbis
funera, cum tumulum praeterlabere recentem!
Nec puer Iliaca quisquam de gente Latinos
in tantum spe tollet avos, nec Romula quondam
ullo se tantum tellus iactabit alumno.
Heu pietas, heu prisca fides invictaque bello
dextera! Non illi se quisquam impune tulisset
obvius armato, seu cum pedes iret in hostem
seu spumantis equi foderet calcaribus armos.
Heu, miserande puer, si qua fata aspera rumpas—
tu Marcellus eris. Manibus date lilia plenis
purpureos spargam flores animamque nepotis
his saltem accumulem donis, et fungar inani
munere." Sic tota passim regione vagantur
aeris in campis latis atque omnia lustrant.
Quae postquam Anchises natum per singula duxit
incenditque animum famae venientis amore,
exim bella viro memorat quae deinde gerenda,
Laurentesque docet populos urbemque Latini,
et quo quemque modo fugiatque feratque laborem.
Sunt geminae Somni portae, quarum altera fertur
cornea, qua veris facilis datur exitus umbris,
altera candenti perfecta nitens elephanto,
sed falsa ad caelum mittunt insomnia Manes.
His ibi tum natum Anchises unaque Sibyllam
prosequitur dictis portaque emittit eburna,
ille viam secat ad naves sociosque revisit.
Tum se ad Caietae recto fert limite portum.
Ancora de prora iacitur; stant litore puppes.

Comprehension Questions

1. In Anchises' prophecy about the accomplishments of the Greeks and Romans (lines 847–53), what does he say the Greeks will be especially good at? The Romans?

2. Vergil has Anchises emphasize the elder Marcellus' military prowess. Why does Vergil do this?

____

____

____

3. What can we infer about the younger Marcellus from Aeneas' questions and comments in lines 863–66? ____

____

____

____

____

____

____

4. What does Anchises say was the gods' reason for having Marcellus die so young?__________

____

____

____

____

5. Marcellus died too young to achieve much in life. What would have been his strength, according to Anchises, if death had not come so early? ______________________________

____

____

____

____

____

6. Why does Anchises call his "duty" (*munere,* line 886) "useless" (*inani,* line 885)? __________

____

____

7. How do lines 890–92 recall the role Anchises played in Book III? ______________________

8. Vergil describes the two gates of sleep, and says that Aeneas and the Sibyl left by the ivory one (lines 893–98). People have posited many reasons for this; what idea do you think Vergil was expressing with this detail? ______________________

Multiple Choice Questions *Suggested time: 15 minutes*

Choose the better answer.

1. The *alii* in line 847 are
   a. Greeks
   b. Romans

2. The word *mollius* (line 847) is an
   a. adjective
   b. adverb

3. In line 849, *-que* connects
   a. *melius* and *meatus*
   b. *orabunt* and *describent*

4. In line 853, *subiectis* is
   a. dative
   b. ablative

5. *Marcellus* (line 855) died
   a. in the third century BCE
   b. in the first century BCE

6. Marcellus acquired the *spolia opima* (line 855) by
   a. leading skirmishes against the Carthaginian general Hannibal
   b. killing the Gallic chief Viridomarus in hand-to-hand combat

7. Marcellus defeated the *Poenos* (line 858) in the war against
   a. the Gallic invaders
   b. the Carthaginians

8. *Quirino* (line 859) is another name for
   a. Romulus
   b. Jupiter

9. The word *parum* (line 862) is an
   a. adverb
   b. adjective

10. In line 865 *circa* here is a(n)
   a. adverb
   b. preposition

11. The first four feet of line 868 scan
   a. dactyl-spondee-spondee-spondee
   b. spondee-spondee-spondee-spondee

12. The case of *propago* (line 870) is
   a. nominative
   b. ablative

13. The form of *esse* needed to complete the verb form *visa* (line 871) is
   a. *sit*
   b. *esset*

14. The word *fuissent* (line 871) is part of a
   a. past contrary-to-fact condition
   b. present contrary-to-fact condition

15. The form of *praeterlabere* (line 874) is
   a. future indicative
   b. imperative

16. In line 877, *tellus* is
   a. genitive
   b. nominative

17. In line 880, *armato* is
   a. ablative
   b. dative

18. In line 882, *qua* is

    a. ablative feminine
    b. accusative neuter

19. The form of *spargam* (line 884) is

    a. present subjunctive
    b. future indicative

20. The number of elisions in line 885 is

    a. zero
    b. one

21. In line 888, *quae* is

    a. accusative plural neuter
    b. nominative singular feminine

22. The form of *esse* needed to complete the verb form *gerenda* (line 890) is

    a. *erant*
    b. *sint*

23. In line 892, *ferat* is subjunctive in a(n)

    a. purpose clause
    b. indirect question

24. Line 894 contains an example of

    a. synecdoche
    b. chiasmus

25. *Caietae* (line 900) is on the

    a. western coast of Italy
    b. eastern edge of Sicily

Translation *Suggested time: 20 minutes*

Translate the following passage as literally as possible.

Sunt geminae Somni portae, quarum altera fertur
cornea, qua veris facilis datur exitus umbris,
altera candenti perfecta nitens elephanto,
sed falsa ad caelum mittunt insomnia Manes.
His ibi tum natum Anchises unaque Sibyllam
prosequitur dictis portaque emittit eburna,
ille viam secat ad naves sociosque revisit.

Scansion

Scan the following lines.

his ibi tum natum Anchises unaque Sibyllam
prosequitur dictis portaque emittit eburna,
ille viam secat ad naves sociosque revisit.
Tum se ad Caietae recto fert limite portum.

(lines 897–900)

Book VI Comprehensive Review Essay

At several points in the *Aeneid,* Aeneas encounters characters who give him crucial advice. Sibyl is one example. Identify three other such characters from the first half of the *Aeneid* and discuss the role they play in helping Aeneas make his way to Italy. Present your response in a well-organized essay.

Support your assertions with references drawn from the first half of the *Aeneid.* Please write your essay on a separate piece of paper.

THE *AENEID*
BOOK X SELECTIONS
WITH EXERCISES

LESSON 28: BOOK X. 420–509

. . . Quem sic Pallas petit ante precatus:
"Da nunc, Thybri pater, ferro, quod missile libro,
fortunam atque viam duri per pectus Halaesi.
haec arma exuviasque viri tua quercus habebit."
Audiit illa deus; dum texit Imaona Halaesus,
Arcadio infelix telo dat pectus inermum.
At non caede viri tanta perterrita Lausus,
pars ingens belli, sinit agmina: primus Abantem
oppositum interimit, pugnae nodumque moramque.
Sternitur Arcadiae proles, sternuntur Etrusci
et vos, o Grais imperdita corpora, Teucri.
Agmina concurrunt ducibusque et viribus aequis;
extremi addensent acies nec turba moveri
tela manusque sinit. Hinc Pallas instat et urget,
hinc contra Lausus, nec multum discrepat aetas,
egregii forma, sed quis Fortuna negarat
in patriam reditus. Ipsos concurrere passus
haud tamen inter se magni regnator Olympi;
mox illos sua fata manent maiore sub hoste.
Interea soror alma monet succedere Lauso
Turnum, qui volucri curru medium secat agmen.
Ut vidit socios: "Tempus desistere pugnae;
solus ego in Pallanta feror, soli mihi Pallas
debetur; cuperem ipse parens spectator adesset."
Haec ait, et socii cesserunt aequore iusso.
At Rutulum abscessu iuvenis tum iussa superba
miratus stupet in Turno corpusque per ingens
lumina volvit obitque truci procul omnia visu,
talibus et dictis it contra dicta tyranni:
"Aut spoliis ego iam raptis laudabor opimis
aut leto insigni: sorti pater aequus utrique est.
Tolle minas." Fatus medium procedit in aequor;
frigidus Arcadibus coit in praecordia sanguis.
Desiluit Turnus biiugis, pedes apparat ire
comminus; utque leo, specula cum vidit ab alta
stare procul campis meditantem in proelia taurum,
advolat, haud alia est Turni venientis imago.
Hunc ubi contiguum missae fore credidit hastae,
ire prior Pallas, si qua fors adiuvet ausum
viribus imparibus, magnumque ita ad aethera fatur:
"Per patris hospitium et mensas, quas advena adisti,
te precor, Alcide, coeptis ingentibus adsis.
Cernat semineci sibi me rapere arma cruenta

victoremque ferant morientia lumina Turni."
Audiit Alcides iuvenem magnumque sub imo
corde premit gemitum lacrimasque effundit inanes.
Tum genitor natum dictis adfatur amicis:
"Stat sua cuique dies, breve et inreparabile tempus
omnibus est vitae; sed famam extendere factis,
hoc virtutis opus. Troiae sub moenibus altis
tot gnati cecidere deum, quin occidit una
Sarpedon, mea progenies; etiam sua Turnum
fata vocant metasque dati pervenit ad aevi."
Sic ait, atque oculos Rutulorum reicit arvis.
At Pallas magnis emittit viribus hastam
vaginaque cava fulgentem deripit ensem.
Illa volans umeri surgunt qua tegmina summa
incidit, atque viam clipei molita per oras
tandem etiam magno strinxit de corpore Turni.
Hic Turnus ferro praefixum robur acuto
in Pallanta diu librans iacit atque ita fatur:
"Aspice num mage sit nostrum penetrabile telum."
Dixerat; at clipeum, tot ferri terga, tot aeris,
quem pellis totiens obeat circumdata tauri,
vibranti cuspis medium transverberat ictu
loricaeque moras et pectus perforat ingens.
Ille rapit calidum frustra de vulnere telum:
una eademque via sanguis animusque sequuntur.
Corruit in vulnus (sonitum super arma dedere)
et terram hostilem moriens petit ore cruento.
Quem Turnus super adsistens:
"Arcades, haec" inquit "memores mea dicta referte
Evandro: qualem meruit, Pallanta remitto.
Quisquis honos tumuli, quidquid solamen humandi est,
largior. Haud illi stabunt Aeneia parvo
hospitia." Et laevo pressit pede talia fatus
exanimem rapiens immania pondera baltei
impressumque nefas: una sub nocte iugali
caesa manus iuvenum foede thalamique cruenti,
quae Clonus Eurytides multo caelaverat auro;
quo nunc Turnus ovat spolio gaudetque potitus.
Nescia mens hominum fati sortisque futurae
et servare modum rebus sublata secundis!
Turno tempus erit magno cum optaverit emptum
intactum Pallanta, et cum spolia ista diemque
oderit. At socii multo gemitu lacrimisque
impositum scuto referunt Pallanta frequentes.
O dolor atque decus magnum rediture parenti,
haec te prima dies bello dedit, haec eadem aufert,
cum tamen ingentes Rutulorum linquis acervos!

Comprehension Questions

1. Why are the troops (line 427) described as *perterrita*? How does this detail develop the characterization of Pallas? ______________________________

____

____

____

2. How does Vergil show Lausus' military prowess in lines 426–30? Provide line references in parentheses for your Latin choices.

____

____

____

____

____

3. In lines 433–35, how does Vergil show that Pallas and Lausus would have been fairly matched in a fight? ______________________________

____

____

____

____

4. How is Turnus' cruelty shown in line 443? Whom in Book II does this sentiment recall?

____

____

____

____

____

5. In contrast to Lausus and Pallas, Turnus and Pallas are unevenly matched. How does Vergil show this in lines 445–56?

6. Why does Pallas pray to Hercules?

7. What aspect of Turnus' character is emphasized by his despoiling Pallas of his baldric?

8. What warning about human nature is implied in line 502?

9. What is the effect of the apostrophe in line 507?

Multiple Choice Questions *Suggested time: 36 minutes*

1. The word *quem* (line 420) refers to
   a. the Tiber
   b. Halaesus
   c. Aeneas
   d. Jupiter

2. The case and number of *perterrita* (line 426) is
   a. nominative singular
   b. ablative singular
   c. nominative plural
   d. accusative plural

3. *pars* in line 427 is in apposition to
   a. *caede* (line 426)
   b. *viri* (line 426)
   c. *Lausus* (line 426)
   d. *agmina* (line 427)

4. Line 430 contains an example of
   a. apostrophe
   b. hendiadys
   c. synchysis
   d. enallage

5. The subject of *addensent* (line 432) is
   a. *extremi* (line 432)
   b. *acies* (line 432)
   c. *turba* (line 432)
   d. *manus* (line 433)

6. The case of *quis* (line 435) is
   a. nominative
   b. genitive
   c. dative
   d. accusative

7. In line 435, *negarat* is
   a. present indicative
   b. present subjunctive
   c. perfect indicative
   d. pluperfect indicative

8. The *soror* mentioned in line 439 is
   a. Allecto
   b. Juturna
   c. Amata
   d. Lavinia

9. The case of *soli* (line 442) is
   a. nominative
   b. genitive
   c. dative
   d. ablative

10. In line 443, Turnus wishes that
    a. Evander were present
    b. there were more spectators
    c. he could see Latinus
    d. his father would come

11. Line 444 contains an example of
   a. hysteron proteron
   b. polysyndeton
   c. zeugma
   d. enallage

12. The case of *Rutulum* (line 445) is
   a. nominative
   b. genitive
   c. accusative
   d. ablative

13. In line 447, *visu* is a(n)
   a. supine
   b. adjective
   c. noun
   d. participle

14. The phrase *sorti . . . utrique* (line 450) refers to
   a. Pallas/Turnus
   b. spoils/death
   c. father/son
   d. war/defeat

15. The metrical pattern of the first four feet of line 453 is
   a. dactyl-spondee-dactyl-dactyl
   b. dactyl-dactyl-dactyl-spondee
   c. dactyl-dactyl-spondee-dactyl
   d. spondee-dactyl-dactyl-dactyl

16. *Alcide* (line 461) is a patronymic for
   a. Hercules
   b. Ascanius
   c. Evander
   d. Turnus

17. In line 462, *sibi* refers to
   a. Alcides
   b. Pallas
   c. *advena*
   d. Turnus

18. In lines 467–69, Jupiter says that
   a. the time left in the battle is short, so Turnus will have to act with courage
   b. each day brings its own trials, but we must nevertheless think of what is right
   c. the lifespan of everyone is short, and some people live by words but others by action
   d. all must die, but our actions can lengthen how long we are remembered after we die

19. Line 472 contains an example of
   a. chiasmus
   b. tmesis
   c. anastrophe
   d. hiatus

20. The word *illa* (line 476) refers to
   a. *hastam* (line 474)
   b. *vagina* (line 475)
   c. *ensem* (line 475)
   d. *tegmina* (line 476)

21. Line 479 contains an example of
    a. asyndeton
    b. chiasmus
    c. hyperbaton
    d. synchysis

22. The number of elisions in line 481 is
    a. zero
    b. one
    c. two
    d. three

23. In line 487,
    a. Turnus pursues Pallas
    b. Pallas dies
    c. the path becomes bloody
    d. Pallas pulls out the spear

24. Line 487 contains
    a. hiatus
    b. synizesis
    c. a fifth foot spondee
    d. tmesis

25. *Evandro* (line 492) is Pallas's
    a. son
    b. best friend
    c. commander
    d. father

26. Lines 497–98 (*una . . . cruenti*) refer to the
    a. Danaids' slaughter of their husbands
    b. death of Dido
    c. marriage of Peleus and Thetis
    d. end of Priam's lineage

27. The case and number of *manus* (line 498) is
    a. nominative singular
    b. genitive singular
    c. nominative plural
    d. accusative plural

28. In line 502, *servare* is a(n)
    a. imperative
    b. indicative
    c. infinitive
    d. participle

29. The tense and mood of *optaverit* (line 503) is
    a. imperfect subjunctive
    b. future perfect indicative
    c. perfect subjunctive
    d. future indicative

30. In line 507, *rediture* is a(n)
    a. second person indicative
    b. ablative noun
    c. imperative
    d. vocative participle

Translation *Suggested time: 20 minutes*

Translate the following passage as literally as possible.

Hunc ubi contiguum missae fore credidit hastae,
ire prior Pallas, si qua fors adiuvet ausum
viribus imparibus, magnumque ita ad aethera fatur:
"Per patris hospitium et mensas, quas advena adisti,
te precor, Alcide, coeptis ingentibus adsis.
Cernat semineci sibi me rapere arma cruenta
victoremque ferant morientia lumina Turni."

Scansion

Scan the following lines.

"aut spoliis ego iam raptis laudabor opimis
aut leto insigni: sorti pater aequus utrique est.
Tolle minas." Fatus medium procedit in aequor;

(lines 449–51)

Two trickier ones:

una eademque via sanguis animusque sequuntur (line 487)
Evandro: qualem meruit, Pallanta remitto (line 492)

Book X Comprehensive Review Essay

Scenes involving compassion (or a lack thereof) are used repeatedly by Vergil in the *Aeneid* to develop both human and divine characterization in the poem. In this episode from Book 10, Turnus' lack of compassion for Pallas is observed by both Jupiter and Hercules. How does their reaction contribute to the characterization of Turnus, and what does it suggest about the role of compassion in the poem as a whole?

Support your assertions with references drawn from **throughout** this passage (lines 420–509 only). All Latin words must be copied or their line numbers provided, AND they must be translated or paraphrased closely enough so that it is clear you understand the Latin. It is your responsibility to convince your reader that you are basing your conclusions on the Latin text and not merely on a general recollection of the passage. Direct your answer to the question; do not merely summarize the passage. Please write your essay on a separate piece of paper.

Latin

SUCKS

THE *AENEID* BOOK XII SELECTIONS WITH EXERCISES

LESSON 29: BOOK XII. 791–842

Iunonem interea rex omnipotentis Olympi
adloquitur fulva pugnas de nube tuentem:
"Quae iam finis erit, coniunx? Quid denique restat?
Indigetem Aenean scis ipsa et scire fateris
deberi caelo fatisque ad sidera tolli.
Quid struis? Aut qua spe gelidis in nubibus haeres?
Mortalin decuit violari vulnere divum?
Aut ensem (quid enim sine te Iuturna valeret?)
ereptum reddi Turno et vim crescere victis?
Desine iam tandem precibusque inflectere nostris,
ne te tantus edit tacitam dolor et mihi curae
saepe tuo dulci tristes ex ore recursent.
Ventum ad supremum est. Terris agitare vel undis
Troianos potuisti, infandum accendere bellum,
deformare domum et luctu miscere hymenaeos:
ulterius temptare veto." Sic Iuppiter orsus;
sic dea summisso contra Saturnia vultu:
"Ista quidem quia nota mihi tua, magne, voluntas,
Iuppiter, et Turnum et terras invita reliqui;
nec tu me aëria solam nunc sede videres
digna indigna pati, sed flammis cincta sub ipsa
starem acie traheremque inimica in proelia Teucros.
Iuturnam misero (fateor) succurrere fratri
suasi et pro vita maiora audere probavi,
non ut tela tamen, non ut contenderet arcum;
adiuro Stygii caput implacabile fontis,
una superstitio superis quae reddita divis.
Et nunc cedo equidem pugnasque exosa relinquo.
Illud te, nulla fati quod lege tenetur,
pro Latio obtestor, pro maiestate tuorum:
cum iam conubiis pacem felicibus (esto)
component, cum iam leges et foedera iungent,
ne vetus indigenas nomen mutare Latinos
neu Troas fieri iubeas Teucrosque vocari
aut vocem mutare viros aut vertere vestem.
Sit Latium, sint Albani per saecula reges,
sit Romana potens Itala virtute propago:
occidit, occideritque sinas cum nomine Troia."
Olli subridens hominum rerumque repertor:
"Es germana Iovis Saturnique altera proles,

irarum tantos volvis sub pectore fluctus.
Verum age et inceptum frustra summitte furorem:
do quod vis, et me victusque volensque remitto.
Sermonem Ausonii patrium moresque tenebunt,
utque est nomen erit; commixti corpore tantum
subsident Teucri. Morem ritusque sacrorum
adiciam faciamque omnes uno ore Latinos.
Hinc genus Ausonio mixtum quod sanguine surget,
supra homines, supra ire deos pietate videbis,
nec gens ulla tuos aeque celebrabit honores."
Adnuit his Iuno et mentem laetata retorsit;
interea excedit caelo nubemque relinquit.

Comprehension Questions

1. In Jupiter's speech to Juno, about what does he chide her (lines 797–99)? ____________________

____

____

2. What accomplishments of Juno does Jupiter list before he forbids her to try anything further (lines 803–6)? ____

____

____

____

3. What does Juno say she would be doing if she were not respecting Jupiter's will? ____________

____

____

____

4. What is it that Juno swears she did not do? ____________________________________

____

____

5. In lines 821–28, Juno concedes that she will no longer harrass the Trojans, but she makes requests of Jupiter in exchange. What are those requests?

____

____

____

____

____

6. What does Jupiter say he will do in addition to granting Juno's wishes? ______________

____

____

____

Short Answer Questions

Complete the statement or answer the question.

1. *tuentem* (line 792) modifies ______________
2. The subject of *deberi* (line 795) is ______________
3. *ereptum* (line 799) modifies ______________
4. What two items does *–que* (line 800) connect? ______________
5. In what type of clause is *recursent* (line 802)? ______________
6. The part of speech of *ulterius* (line 806) is ______________
7. In line 808, the case of *magne* is ______________
8. The form of *pati* (line 811) is ______________
9. *fratri* (line 813) is dative because ______________
10. The figure of speech that occurs in line 816 is ______________
11. *nulla* (line 819) modifies ______________
12. The tense and mood of *component* (line 822) is ______________
13. *potens* (line 827) modifies ______________
14. The subject of *occiderit* (line 828) is ______________
15. *olli* (line 829) is an archaic form of ______________
16. In line 832, *inceptum* modifies ______________

17. *ut* (line 835) is translated ______________________

18. The figure of speech that occurs in line 837 is ______________________

19. The figure of speech that occurs in line 839 is ______________________

20. *laetata* (line 841) modifies ______________________

Translation *Suggested time: 20 minutes*

Translate the following passage as literally as possible.

Illud te, nulla fati quod lege tenetur,
pro Latio obtestor, pro maiestate tuorum:
cum iam conubiis pacem felicibus (esto)
component, cum iam leges et foedera iungent,
ne vetus indigenas nomen mutare Latinos
neu Troas fieri iubeas Teucrosque vocari
aut vocem mutare viros aut vertere vestem.

____

____

____

____

____

____

____

____

Translation and Analysis Questions

Translate the Latin used in the question and answer the question.

1. What theme of the *Aeneid* is emphasized in lines 794–95, *indigetem Aenean scis ipsa et scire fateris/ deberi caelo fatisque ad sidera tolli?* ______________________

____

____

____

2. What does line 800, *desine iam tandem precibusque inflectere nostris,* show about the relationship between Jupiter and Juno? ______________________________

____

____

3. What does Jupiter mean by *ventum ad supremum est* (line 803)? ______________________________

____

____

4. To what is Jupiter referring in the phrase, *luctu miscere hymenaeos* (line 805)? What phrase in Juno's speech contrasts with this one? ______________________________

____

____

____

5. What does Juno mean by *digna indigna pati* (line 811)? What things might she consider *digna? indigna?* ______________________________

____

____

____

6. Why, in line 824, does Juno request *neu Troas fieri iubeas Teucrosque vocari?* ______________________________

____

____

7. Why does Jupiter characterize all of Juno's efforts as delineated in line 832, *inceptum frustra summitte furorem?* ______________________________

____

____

____

8. How does the prophecy in line 839, *supra homines, supra ire deos pietate videbis,* reflect both Aeneas' character and Augustus'?______________________________

____

____

____

____

Essay *Suggested time: 20 minutes*

This passage presents the last of several important scenes in the *Aeneid* in which two divinities negotiate a mutually agreeable compromise. Identify three other such scenes, and compare the resolution of each. Does this comparison suggest that the outcome of this scene is permanent? Present your response in a well-organized essay. Please write your essay on a separate piece of paper.

Scansion

Scan the following lines.

starem acie traheremque inimica in proelia Teucros.

Iuturnam misero (fateor) succurrere fratri

suasi et pro vita maiora audere probavi,

non ut tela tamen, non ut contenderet arcum;

(lines 812–15)

LESSON 30: BOOK XII. 887–952

Aeneas instat contra telumque coruscat
ingens arboreum, et saevo sic pectore fatur:
"Quae nunc deinde mora est? Aut quid iam, Turne, retractas?
Non cursu, saevis certandum est comminus armis.
Verte omnes tete in facies et contrahe quidquid
sive animis sive arte vales; opta ardua pennis
astra sequi clausumque cava te condere terra."
Ille caput quassans: "Non me tua fervida terrent
dicta, ferox; di me terrent et Iuppiter hostis."
Nec plura effatus saxum circumspicit ingens,
saxum antiquum ingens, campo quod forte iacebat,
limes agro positus litem ut discerneret arvis.
Vix illum lecti bis sex cervice subirent,
qualia nunc hominum producit corpora tellus;
ille manu raptum trepida torquebat in hostem
altior insurgens et cursu concitus heros.
Sed neque currentem se nec cognoscit euntem
tollentemve manu saxumve immane moventem;
genua labant, gelidus concrevit frigore sanguis.
Tum lapis ipse viri vacuum per inane volutus
nec spatium evasit totum neque pertulit ictum.
Ac velut in somnis, oculos ubi languida pressit
nocte quies, nequiquam avidos extendere cursus
velle videmur et in mediis conatibus aegri
succidimus; non lingua valet, non corpore notae
sufficiunt vires nec vox aut verba sequuntur:
sic Turno, quacumque viam virtute petivit,
successum dea dira negat. Tum pectore sensus
vertuntur varii; Rutulos aspectat et urbem
cunctaturque metu letumque instare tremescit,
nec quo se eripiat, nec qua vi tendat in hostem,
nec currus usquam videt aurigamve sororem.
Cunctanti telum Aeneas fatale coruscat,
sortitus fortunam oculis, et corpore toto
eminus intorquet. Murali concita numquam
tormento sic saxa fremunt nec fulmine tanti
dissultant crepitus. Volat atri turbinis instar
exitium dirum hasta ferens orasque recludit
loricae et clipei extremos septemplicis orbes;
per medium stridens transit femur. Incidit ictus
ingens ad terram duplicato poplite Turnus.
Consurgunt gemitu Rutuli totusque remugit

mons circum et vocem late nemora alta remittunt.
Ille humilis supplex oculos dextramque precantem
protendens "Equidem merui nec deprecor" inquit;
"utere sorte tua. Miseri te si qua parentis
tangere cura potest, oro (fuit et tibi talis
Anchises genitor) Dauni miserere senectae
et me, seu corpus spoliatum lumine mavis,
redde meis. Vicisti et victum tendere palmas
Ausonii videre; tua est Lavinia coniunx,
ulterius ne tende odiis." Stetit acer in armis
Aeneas volvens oculos dextramque repressit;
et iam iamque magis cunctantem flectere sermo
coeperat, infelix umero cum apparuit alto
balteus et notis fulserunt cingula bullis
Pallantis pueri, victum quem vulnere Turnus
straverat atque umeris inimicum insigne gerebat.
Ille, oculis postquam saevi monimenta doloris
exuviasque hausit, furiis accensus et ira
terribilis: "Tune hinc spoliis indute meorum
eripiare mihi? Pallas te hoc vulnere, Pallas
immolat et poenam scelerato ex sanguine sumit."
Hoc dicens ferrum adverso sub pectore condit
fervidus; ast illi solvuntur frigore membra
vitaque cum gemitu fugit indignata sub umbras.

Comprehension Questions

1. What does Aeneas say Turnus should hope for? ____________________

____

____

2. What does Turnus say he fears more than Aeneas' words? ____________________

____

____

3. What is the effect of the anaphora in lines 896–97? ____________________

____

____

4. What happens to Turnus when he throws the rock? ____________________

____

____

5. How does the simile in lines 908–12 highlight the action of the narrative? ______

6. Who is the *dira dea* (line 914)? ______

7. How does Vergil show Turnus' feelings in lines 914–18? ______

8. How does Vergil emphasize Aeneas' martial skill in lines 919–26? ______

9. What request does Turnus make of Aeneas? ______

10. Why does Aeneas hesitate in line 940? ______

11. Why does Pallas' baldric infuriate Aeneas? ______

12. Who does Aeneas say is killing Turnus? Why? ______

Short Answer Questions

Complete the statement or answer the question.

1. In line 888, *arboreum* modifies ____________________
2. The form of *sequi* (line 893) is ____________________
3. *ingens* (line 896) modifies ____________________
4. In line 897, *forte* is translated ____________________
5. *subirent* (line 899) is subjunctive in what type of incompleted condition? ____________________
6. In line 901, *ille* refers to ____________________
7. *ipse* (line 906) modifies ____________________
8. *languida* (line 908) modifies ____________________
9. The case of *sensus* (line 914) is ____________________
10. In line 917, *eripiat* is subjunctive in what type of clause? ____________________
11. What figure of speech is used in lines 921–23? ____________________
12. The case of *crepitus* (line 923) is ____________________
13. The number of elisions in line 929 is ____________________
14. *sorte* (line 932) is ablative because ____________________
15. The form of *miserere* (line 934) is ____________________
16. The part of speech of *ulterius* (line 938) is ____________________
17. The subject of *fulserunt* (line 942) is ____________________
18. *victum* (line 943) modifies ____________________
19. The form of *eripiare* (line 948) is ____________________
20. *indignata* (line 952) modifies ____________________

Translation *Suggested time: 10 minutes*

Translate the following passage as literally as possible.

Sed neque currentem se nec cognoscit euntem
tollentemve manu saxumve immane moventem;
genua labant, gelidus concrevit frigore sanguis.
Tum lapis ipse viri vacuum per inane volutus
nec spatium evasit totum neque pertulit ictum.

____

____

____

____

____

____

Translation and Analysis Questions

Translate any Latin used in the question and answer the question.

1. What do lines 899–900, *vix illum lecti bis sex cervice subirent,/ qualia nunc hominum producit corpora tellus,* tell us about how men today compare with men of the past? What do they say about Turnus? ____

____

____

____

____

2. In line 918, *nec currus usquam videt aurigamve sororem,* why would Turnus be looking for his sister?

____

____

____

3. Where else in the *Aeneid* has the theme expressed in lines 934–36, *Dauni miserere senectae/ et me, seu corpus spoliatum lumine mavis,/ redde meis,* arisen? ________________________________

____

____

____

____

4. What exactly is Aeneas feeling in lines 946–47, *furiis accensus et ira/ terribilis*? What has caused this feeling? ____

____

____

____

____

5. Where else was the phrase, *solvuntur frigore membra* (line 951) used? Why does Vergil repeat it here? ____

____

____

____

____

____

Essay *Suggested time: 20 minutes*

In the battle between Turnus and Pallas in Book 10, Vergil emphasized how the two combatants were mismatched. In this lesson's passage, how does he show that Turnus and Aeneas are equally matched? Present your response in a well-organized essay.

Support your assertions with references drawn from **throughout** the passage. All Latin words must be copied or their line numbers provided, AND they must be translated or paraphrased closely enough so that it is clear you understand the Latin. It is your responsibility to convince your reader that you are basing your conclusions on the Latin text and not merely on a general recollection of the passage. Direct your answer to the question; do not merely summarize the passage. Please write your essay on a separate piece of paper.

Scansion

Scan the following lines

Cunctanti telum Aeneas fatale coruscat,

sortitus fortunam oculis, et corpore toto (lines 919–20)

Ille humilis supplex oculos dextramque precantem

protendens "equidem merui nec deprecor" inquit (lines 930–931)

Book XII Comprehensive Review Essay

Compare the heroism of Turnus and Aeneas as displayed in Book XII. Which hero is more sympathetic and why? Present your response in a well-organized essay. Please write your essay on a separate piece of paper.

VOCABULARY

A

ā, ab, abs (away) from, by *(abl.)*

ac, atque and, also; as, than

accipiō, -ere, -cēpī, -ceptus receive, ACCEPT; learn, hear, conceive

Acestēs, -ae, *m.* king in Sicily

āctus, -a, -um *see* **agō**

ad to, toward, at, near, about *(acc.)*

adfore; adforem, -ēs, -et *see* **adsum**

adsum, -esse, -fuī be present, assist *(dat.)*

Aenēās, -ae, *acc.* **-ān,** *m.* Trojan prince, son of Venus and Anchises, hero of the *Aeneid*

aequor, aequoris, *n.* sea, waves; (level) plain

age, agite (agō) up! come! lead on!

agmen, agminis, *n.* army, line, troop; course

agō, -ere, ēgī, āctus lead, drive, do, treat, pass, conduct

aiō, ais, ait; aiunt say, speak, assert

alius, -a, -ud other, another, else

altus, -a, -um (on) high, lofty, deep

amor, amōris, *m.* love, desire, passion

Anchīsēs, -ae, *acc.* **-ēn,** *m.* Trojan prince, father of Aeneas

anima, -ae, *f.* air, breath, life, soul, shade

animus, -ī, *m.* soul, spirit, breath, courage; anger, pride; purpose, thought

ante before *(acc.)*; sooner, previously

antīquus, -a, -um ANCIENT, old, aged, former, of olden times, time-honored

āra, -ae, *f.* altar

ardeō, -ēre, arsī, arsus burn, be eager

arma, -ōrum, *n. pl.* ARMS, equipment, tools

arvum, -ī, *n.* plowed land, field, region

arx, arcis, *f.* citadel, fort; height, hill

at, ast but, yet, however, at least

āter, ātra, ātrum black, gloomy, deadly

atque, ac and, also; as, then

audiō, -īre, -īvī (-iī), -ītus hear (of), hearken

aura, -ae, *f.* breeze, air; favor; light

aurum, -ī, *n.* gold (object, equipment)

aut or, either; **aut . . . aut** either . . . or

B

bellum, -ī, *n.* war(fare), combat, fight

C

caelum, -ī, *n.* sky, heaven; weather

campus, -ī, *m.* plain, field, level surface

capiō, -ere, cēpī, captus take, seize, catch; CAPTIVATE; deceive; occupy

caput, capitis, *n.* head; summit; life, person

cāsus, -ūs, *m.* chance, (mis)fortune; fall

cernō, -ere, crēvī, crētus DISCERN, perceive, understand, decide; fight

circum around, about, at, near *(acc.)*

clāmor, clāmōris, *m.* shout, roar, applause

classis, classis, *f.* fleet, army, ship

comes, comitis, *m.* *(f.)* comrade, follower

coniūnx, coniugis, *m.* *(f.)* husband, wife

corpus, corporis, *n.* body, CORPSE, form

cum *(conj.)* when, while, since, although

cum *(prep.)* with *(abl.)*

cūnctus, -a, -um all, whole, entire

cūra, -ae, *f.* care, anxiety, grief; love

cursus, -ūs, *m.* COURSE, running; haste

D

Danaus, -a, -um Danaan, Greek

dē (down, away) from, of, concerning, according to *(abl.)*

dea, -ae, *f.* goddess

deus, -ī, *m.* god, divinity, DEITY

dexter, -(e)ra, -(e)rum right (hand); favorable; *f. subst.* right hand

dīcō, -ere, dīxī, dictus say, speak, tell, call, name, describe, chant

dictum, -ī, *n.* word, speech, command

Dīdō, Didōnis, *f.* legendary founder and queen of Carthage

diēs, diēī, *m. (f.)* DAY, time, season

dīvus, -a, -um DIVINE, heavenly, deified; *subst.* DIVINITY, god, goddess

dō, dare, dedī, datus give (forth), grant, allow, bestow; put, place, make

domus, -ūs, *f.* house(hold), home, abode; family, race, line

dōnum, -ī, *n.* gift, offering, prize, reward

dūcō, -ere, dūxī, ductus lead, draw (out), protract; PRODUCE; think

dum while, as long as, until, provided

E

ē, ex out of, from, according to *(abl.)*

ēgī *see* **agō**

ego, meī *(pl.* **nōs, nostrum)** I

eō, īre, īvī (iī), itus go, proceed, come

equus, -ī, *m.* horse, steed, charger

ēripiō, -ere, -uī, ēreptus snatch (from), tear away; rescue; hasten

errō, errāre stray, wander, ERR; linger

et and, also, even, too; **et . . . et** both . . . and

euntis, -ī, -em, -e, -ēs, -ium, -ibus *see* **eō**

ex, ē out of, from, according to *(abl.)*

F

faciō, -ere, fēcī, factus do, make, perform; grant, offer; suppose

fāma, -ae, *f.* FAME, report, reputation

fāre, fārī; fātur; fātus, -a, -um *see* **for**

fātum, -ī, *n.* FATE, destiny, doom, oracle

ferō, ferre, tulī, lātus bear, endure; wear; report, say; carry (off), plunder; extol; tend; grant, offer

ferrum, -ī, *n.* iron; sword, weapon, tool

fessus, -a, -um tired, weary, feeble, worn

fīnis, finis, *m. (f.)* end, limit, border; country; goal; starting-place

flamma, -ae, *f.* FLAME, fire, torch; love

flūctus, -ūs, *m.* wave, tide, flood, sea

for, fārī, fātus speak, say, tell, utter

fore; forem, -ēs, -et *see* **sum**

fors, fortis, *f.* chance, FORTUNE, hap

fortūna, -ae, *f.* FORTUNE, chance, luck

fuga, -ae, *f.* flight, haste, exile, speed

fugiō, -ere, fūgī flee (from), escape, shun

fundō, -ere, fūdī, fūsus pour (out), shed; lay low, slay, rout; extend

furō, -ere, uī rage, rave, be frantic

futūrus, -a, -um FUTURE, destined (to be), impending, about to be; *see* **sum**

G

geminus, -a, -um twin, double, two

genitor, genitōris, *m.* begetter, father, sire

gēns, gentis, *f.* clan, race, nation, herd

genus, generis, *n.* birth, origin, race; descendant; kind, family

H

habeō, -ēre, -uī, -itus have, hold; consider

haud not, by no means, not at all

heu alas! ah! ah me!

hīc *(adv.)* here, there, hereupon

hic, haec, hoc this, that; he, she, it

hinc from this place, hence, thence

honōs (or), honōris, *m.* HONOR , glory, reward; offering, sacrifice; charm, grace

hūc to this place, hither, here

I

ī , ībam, ībō, īre, it, īte *see* **eō**

iam now, already, finally, at once

īdem, eadem, idem same, the same

ignis, ignis, *m.* fire, flame, light, lightning, star; passion, love, fury, wrath

ille, illa, illud that (famous); he, she, it

immānis, immāne huge, monstrous, enormous, mighty, dreadful, cruel, atrocious

imperium, -(i)ī, *n.* command, power, dominion, rule, sway, mastery, realm(s)

īmus, -a, -um *superl. of* **īnferus**

in, in, on, in the case of, among *(abl);* into, against, until, toward *(acc.)*

īnfēlīx, īnfēlīcis unfortunate, accursed, unhappy, ill-omened, unlucky, wretched

īnferus, -a, -um low, below, underneath

ingēns, ingentis enormous, mighty, huge

inter between, among, during *(acc.)*

Iovis, -ī, -em, -e *see* **Iuppiter**

ipse, -sa, -sum (him, her, it)-self; very

īra, -ae, *f.* wrath, rage, anger, passion

īre *see* **eō**

is, ea, id this, that; he, she it

it, īte *see* **eō**

Ītalia, -ae, *f.* Italy

iubeō, -ēre, iussi, iussus command, order, bid, enjoin (upon), urge

Iūnō, Iūnōnis, *f.* queen of the gods

Iuppiter, Iovis, *m.* king of the gods

iussī; iussus, -a, -um *see* **iubeō**

L

lābor, lābī, lāpsus slip (by), slide, glide (by), descend; fail; faint; fall, perish; flow

labōs (or), labōris, *m.* LABOR, hardship, task

lacrima, -ae, *f.* tear, compassion

laetus, -a, -um happy; fertile; fat, sleek

līmen, līminis, *n.* threshold, doorway, entrance; abode; shrine; palace

lītus, lītoris, *n.* shore, strand, coast, beach

locus, -ī, *m.* **(***pl.* **locī, loca)** place, region; condition, situation; opportunity

longus, -a, -um long, wide, distant

lūmen, lūminis, *n.* light, lamp; eye; life

lūx, lūcis, *f.* light, sun, day; life; glory

M

magnus, -a, -um great, large, huge, vast; noble, illustrious, mighty, important

maior, maius *compar. of* **magnus**

maneō, -ēre, mānsī, mānsus remain, abide, linger, stay, (a)wait

manus, -ūs, *f.* hand; band, troop; deed

mare, maris, *n.* sea

māter, matris, *f.* mother; MATRON

maximus *superl. of* **magnus**

medius, -a, -um mid(dle), INTERMEDIATE

mēns, mentis, *f.* mind, feeling, intention

meus, -a, -um my (own), mine

miser, misera, miserum MISERABLE, unhappy, wretched, unfortunate, pitiable

mittō, -ere, mīsī, missus send, hurl, DISMISS, let go; end, finish; offer, pay

moenia, moenium, *n.* walls; city; structures

mōns, montis, *m.* MOUNTAIN, height

mors, mortis, *f.* death, destruction, ruin

moveō, -ēre, mōvī, mōtus move; ponder

multus, -a, -um much, many, abundant

mūnus, mūneris, *n.* function, duty; gift

N

nam, namque for; indeed, truly

natus, -ī, *m.* son, child, young

nāvis, nāvis, *f.* ship, boat, vessel, galley

-ne *sign of a question;* whether, or

nē lest, that not, no, not

neque, nec nor, neither, and not; **neque . . . neque** neither . . . nor

nōmen, nōminis, *n.* NAME, fame, renown

nōn not, no

noster, nostra, nostrum our (own), ours

novus, -a, -um NEW, young, strange, late

nox, noctis, *f.* night, darkness; sleep

nūllus, -a, -um none, no, no one

nūmen, nūminis, *n.* divinity, divine power (will, favor, purpose, presence)

nunc (but) now, soon, as it is

O

Ō O! oh! ah!

oculus, -ī, *m.* eye

olle *etc., old forms of* **ille**

omnis, omne all, every, whole, universal

ōra, -ae, *f.* shore, coast, region, border

ōs, ōris, *n.* mouth, face; speech

P

parēns, parentis, *m. (f.)* PARENT, ancestor, father, mother

parō, parāre PREPARE, make (ready)

pars, partis, *f.* PART, portion, share, side

pater, patris, *m.* father, ancestor, sire

patrius, -a, -um PATERNAL, ancestral, native

pectus, pectoris, *n.* breast, heart, soul

pelagus, -ī, *n.* sea, flood, waves

per through, by (means of), over, among, because of, during *(acc.)*

pēs, pedis, *m.* foot; sheet-rope, sheet

petō, -ere, -īvī (iī), -ītus seek, attack, aim (at), ask; scan

pius, -a, -um devoted, loyal, righteous

plūrēs *compar. of* **multus**

plūrimus *superl. of* **multus**

plūs *compar. of* **multus**

poena, -ae, *f.* PUNISHMENT, PENALTY, satisfaction, revenge, vengeance

pōnō, -ere, posuī, pos(i)tus put, place (aside); found, establish; bury

portus, -ūs, *m.* PORT, harbor, haven

possum, posse, potuī be able, can, avail

Priamus, -ī, *m.* Priam, king of Troy

prīmus, -a, -um first, foremost, chief

procul far, at a distance, from afar

puer, -ī, *m.* boy, child; slave

puppis, puppis, *f.* stern; ship, vessel, galley

Q

quaerō, -ere, quaesīvī, quaesītus seek (in vain), miss, inquire, ask, try

-que and, also, even; **-que . . . -que** both . . . and

quī, quae, quod who, which, what, that

quis (qua), quid, (qui, quae, quod) who? which? what? why? any, some(one)

quō to where, where(fore), whereby

quondam (at) some time, formerly, ever

R

referō, -ferre, -tulī, -lātus bear back, restore, carry off; reproduce, renew, recall; RELATE, say; (re)pay

rēgīna, -ae, *f.* queen; *adj.* ROYAL

rēgnum, -ī, *n.* royal power, kingdom, REALM, rule, sway, sovereignty

relinquō, -ere, relīquī, relictus leave, desert, surrender, abandon, RELINQUISH

rēmus, -ī, *m.* oar

rēs, reī, *f.* thing, affair, matter, deed, fact, fortune; state, commonwealth

rēx, rēgis, *m.* king; *adj.* ruling, ROYAL

ruō, -ere, ruī, ru(i)tus fall; rush; sink; plow

S

sacer, sacra, sacrum SACRED, holy, consecrated; accursed; *n. subst.* SACRIFICE, holy implement (object); mystery

sanguis, sanguinis, *m.* blood; race, descendant

saxum, -ī, *n.* stone, rock, reef, cliff, crag

sed but, moreover, however

sēdēs, sēdis, *f.* seat; abode, habitation; bottom; tomb, shrine; place, region

sequor, -ī, secūtus follow, attend, pursue, accompany, seek

servō, servāre OBSERVE, watch; PRESERVE, save, guard, keep, rescue; nurse

sī whether, if (only), in case that

sīc thus, so, in this manner

sīdus, sīderis, *n.* star, constellation, meteor; season, weather; heaven

silva, -ae, *f.* forest, wood(s), tree(s)

simul at the same time, together; **simul (ac, atque)** as soon as

socius, soc(i)ī, *m.* ally, comrade, follower

sōlus, -a, -um alone, only, lonely, SOLE

somnus, -ī *m.* sleep, slumber, dream

stō, -āre, stetī, status stand (fast, up); halt; endure; stick (to), remain

sub (from) under, close (to), beneath, (deep) in, after *(acc., abl.)*

subeō, -īre, -īvī (iī), -itus go under, bear; approach, enter; arise *(dat.)*

sublātus, -a, -um *see* **tollō**

suī (of) himself, herself, itself, themselves; him, her, it , them

sum, esse, fuī, futūrus be, exist

summus *superl. of* **superus**

super above, beyond, left, in addition, upon, concerning, about *(acc., abl.)*

superus, -a, -um upper, higher, above; *subst.* god, divinity

suprēmus, -a, -um *superl. of* **superus**

surgō, -ere, surrēxī, surrēctus raise, (a)rise, spring up, SURGE

sustulī *see* **tollō**

suus, -a, -um his, her, its, their (own)

T

tālis, tāle such, of such sort, the following

tandem at length, finally; pray

tantus, -a, -um so great, so much, so far

tēctum, -ī, *n.* roof; house, home, abode

tellūs, tellūris, *f.* earth, land, country

tēlum, -ī, *n.* weapon; wound, blow

tempus, temporis, *n.* time; occasion, crisis

tendō, -ere, tetendī, tentus stretch; hasten, strive, (EX)TEND, aim; tent

teneō, -ēre, tenuī, tentus have, hold, restrain

terra, -ae, *f.* earth, land, country, soil

Teucrus, -a, -um, Teucrian, Trojan

tollō, -ere, sustulī, sublātus lift, raise, upheave, stir up; remove, destroy

tōtus, -a, -um all, every, whole, full

trahō, -ere, trāxi, tractus drag (out), draw (in), lead, PROTRACT; spend

trīstis, trīste sad, unhappy, dreary, fatal

Troia, -ae, *f.* Troy, a city in Asia Minor

tū, tuī (*pl.* **vōs, vestrum**) you

tulī *see* **ferō**

tum, tunc then, at that time; further

tuus, -a, -um your(s), your own

Tyrius, -a, -um Tyrian, Carthaginian

U

ubi where, when, as soon as

ūllus, -a, -um any, any one

umbra, -ae, *f.* shade, shadow, ghost

umerus, -ī, *m.* shoulder

unda, -ae, *f.* wave, billow, water, sea

ūnus, -a, -um one, only, alone, single

urbs, urbis, *f.* city, town

ut(ī) as, when; that, so that; how

V

vastus, -a, -um desolate, VAST, enormous

vātēs, vātis, *m. (f.)* prophet, seer, bard

-ve, vel or, either, even; **vel . . . vel** either . . . or

velim, velle, vellem *see* **volō**

vēlum, -ī, *n.* cloth, canvas, sail

veniō, -īre, vēnī, ventus come, go

ventus, -ī, *m.* wind, breeze, blast, air

via, -ae, *f.* WAY, road, journey, street

victor, victōris, *m.* VICTOR; *adj.* VICTORIOUS

videō, -ēre, vīdī, vīsus see, perceive; *pass.* be seen, appear, seem (best)

vincō, -ere, vīcī, victus conquer, surpass

vir, -ī, *m.* (real) man; hero; husband

vīrēs *pl.* of **vīs**

vīs, vīs, *f.* force, VIOLENCE, energy

vīta, -ae, *f.* life, soul, spirit

vix scarcely, feebly, with difficulty

vocō, vocāre call, name, address, CONVOKE, INVOKE, invite, challenge

volō, velle, voluī will, wish, be willing

volvō, -ere, volvī, volūtus REVOLVE, (un)roll, roll (round, through); undergo

vōx, vōcis, *f.* VOICE, word, speech, sound

Latin Literature Workbook Series
Workbooks That Work LLWS

Writings of Five Significant Ancient Authors
Now Accessible to College and High School Students

Catullus • Cicero • Horace • Ovid • Vergil

LLWS The *Latin Literature Workbook Series* reinforces practical approaches to reading classical authors in the original.

Sets of exercises that enable the student to quickly reach a higher degree of comprehension and appreciation of sight or prepared passages. Exercises include:

- Short analysis questions
- Translation passages
- Short and long essay questions on literary interpretation
- Lines for scansion
- Short answer questions and multiple choice questions on
  - Grammatical underpinnings of the passage
  - Figures of speech and rhetorical devices
  - Identification of characters, events, places, historical and mythical allusions

Each workbook was written by a team of authors—one, a university scholar with special expertise in the Latin literary text, and the other, a high school Advanced Placement Latin teacher. Because of the double focus of these experts, the series is sensitive to the needs of both college and high school students at the intermediate level.

The pedagogical value of workbooks in foreign language courses has long been recognized. Use this exciting series as mini-textbooks to cover several ancient authors in one college level course, or as an ancillary for individual author courses in high school or college. Watch students learn to read Latin authors with greater ease and pleasure, comprehend and analyze content, and develop skills and interest in literary analysis that allow them to go forward with confidence to courses that require more reading, and at a deeper level. These are "Workbooks that Work" for all students, intermediate level and beyond, both high school (AP* or not) and college.

The TEACHER'S MANUALS • give answers to all exercises • identify salient points for complete answers to short analysis questions • include the "chunking" method of evaluating all translation passages • identify topics essential to full answers for the essay questions • give instructions on how to use the six to one grading rubric • give scansion marks according to meter for select lines of poetic selections.

"Bolchazy-Carducci Publishers is the premier publisher of books and curriculum materials for Latin language and literature studies."

– *Midwest Book Review*

"*A Horace Workbook* is exactly the sort of book I wish I had when I was first starting to decipher Latin poetry. And again, when I was reading Horace in graduate school seminars… [it] has just about the right touch: it uses grammar and other exercises to help you understand the poem, not to test your mastery of minutia… Anybody who has struggled through Latin verse and wished they'd gotten more out of it, should give this workbook a look."

– Geoffrey Barto, Multilingua.info

"*A Horace Workbook* is a very nice resource which should be helpful to both students and teachers alike."

– Thomas Stewart, *The Classical Outlook*

A Horace Workbook
David Murphy & Ronnie Ancona

Student Text: xii + 204 pp. (2005) 8½" x 11" Paperback
ISBN 978-0-86516-574-8
Teacher's Manual: xvi + 274 pp. (2006) 6" x 9" Paperback
ISBN 978-0-86516-649-3

A Vergil Workbook
Katherine Bradley & Barbara Weiden Boyd

Student Text: x + 262 pp. (2006) 8½" x 11" Paperback
ISBN 978-0-86516-614-1
Teacher's Manual: xviii + 302 pp. (2007) 6" x 9" Paperback
ISBN 978-0-86516-651-6

An Ovid Workbook
Charbra Adams Jestin & Phyllis B. Katz

Student Text: x + 166 pp. (2006) 8½" x 11" Paperback
ISBN 978-0-86516-625-7
Teacher Manual: xii + 172 pp. (2007) 6" x 9" Paperback
ISBN 978-0-86516-626-4

A Catullus Workbook
Helena Dettmer & LeaAnn A. Osburn

Student Text: xii + 244 pp. (2006) 8½" x 11" Paperback
ISBN 978-0-86516-623-3
Teacher Manual: xvi + 328 pp. (2007) 6" x 9" Paperback
ISBN 978-0-86516-624-0

A Cicero Workbook
Jane W. Crawford & Judith A. Hayes

Student Text: x + 238 pp. (2006) 8½" x 11" Paperback
ISBN 978-0-86516-643-1
Teacher Manual: xiv + 250 pp. (2007) 6" x 9" Paperback
ISBN 978-0-86516-654-7

*AP is a registered trademark of the College Entrance Examination Board, which was not involved in the production of, and does not endorse, this product.

Bolchazy-Carducci Publishers, Inc.
www.BOLCHAZY.com

VERGIL'S AENEID

Selections from Books 1, 2, 4, 6, 10, and 12, 2nd edition

Barbara Weiden Boyd

This edition is designed for high school Advanced Placement and college level courses: a newly updated and revised version of selected passages from Vergil's *Aeneid, Books I–VI,* by Clyde Pharr. Passages included are: 1.1–519; 2.1–56; 199–297, 469–566, 735–804; 4.1–448, 642–705; 6.1–211, 450–476, 847–901; 10.420–509; 12.791–842, 887–952.

Boyd's textbook will likely attract a loyal following . . .
– Daniel N. Erickson, *The Classical Outlook*

Student Text: (2004, 2nd edition)
Paperback, ISBN 978-0-86516-584-7 • Hardbound, ISBN 978-0-86516-583-0
Teacher's Guide: (2002) Paperback, ISBN 978-0-86516-481-9

VERGIL'S AENEID

8 & 11: Italy & Rome

Barbara Weiden Boyd

This edition features: • Latin text of 395 lines of Vergil's *Aeneid:* 8.608–731 (shield of Aeneas), 11.498–596 (introduction to Camilla), 11.664–835 (Camilla's heroism and defeat), with selected vocabulary and notes on the same page • Glossary of rhetorical terms and figures of speech, following Pharr's popular design • Selected bibliography • Full vocabulary (with macrons)

xi + 96 pp. (2006) 6" x 9" Paperback, ISBN 978-086516-580-9

VERGIL'S AENEID

Books I–VI

Clyde Pharr

Both paperback and clothbound now contain an "Annotated Bibliography on Vergil, to Supplement Pharr's *Aeneid,*" by Alexander McKay, a bibliography of articles and books in English, for use in college and high school Vergil courses, for students and their teachers.

Illus., xvii + 518 pp. + fold-out (1964, Reprint 1998)
Paperback, ISBN 978-086516-421-5 • Hardbound, ISBN 978-086516-433-8

BOLCHAZY-CARDUCCI PUBLISHERS, INC.
WWW.BOLCHAZY.COM

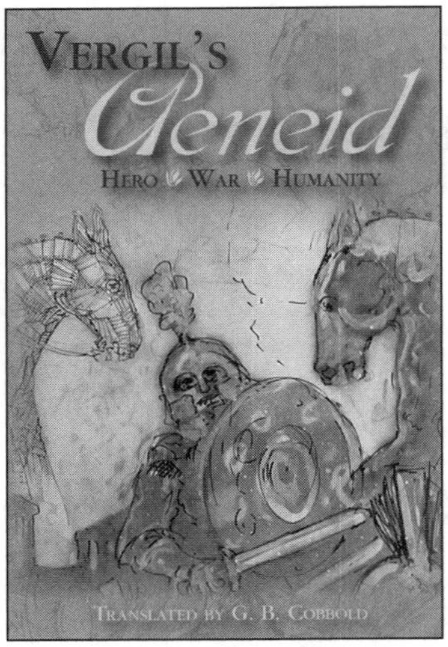

Vergil's Aeneid

Hero • War • Humanity

Translated by G. B. Cobbold

At last the pillar of Western literary tradition is available as a reader-friendly novel that retains the poetic vividness of the original. *Vergil's Aeneid: Hero • War • Humanity* resonates with the challenges of today's world.

This vibrant edition of the *Aeneid* includes sidebar summaries, engaging in-text illustrations, and five indices.

xviii + 366 pp., 91 Illustrations: 12 b&w full-page + 79 b&w in-text; 1 map
(2005) 5" x 7 ¾" Paperback, ISBN 978-0-86516-596-0

Vergil Vocabulary Cards for AP* Selections

Dennis De Young

A Complete Vocabulary, Grammar, and Poetry Reference for AP* and College Vergil Classes

Four invaluable study aids! This set includes: • 587 vocabulary flashcards, divided into three groups (by frequency of occurrence), on perforated cardstock; full Latin vocabulary entry on one side (with macrons, accents, and complete principal parts for verbs and nominative and genitive forms for nouns), English meanings plus select derivatives/cognates on the other side • **full AP* selections vocabulary list • grammatical form summaries,** reproduced from *Graphic Latin Grammar* • **additional quick-reference guide** on Meter, Rhetorical Terms, Figures of Speech, and Rhetorical Devices

250 pp., Perforated cardstock (2005) 8½ " x 11" Paperback, ISBN 978-0-86516-610-3

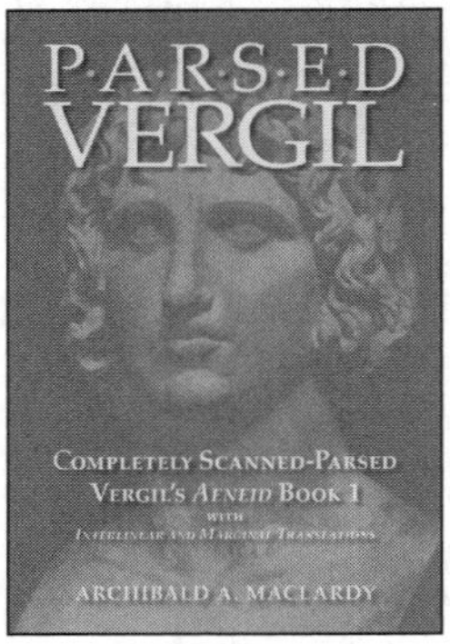

Parsed Vergil: Completely Scanned-Parsed Vergil's *Aeneid* Book I

With Interlinear and Marginal Translations

Archibald A. Maclardy

An irreplaceable, primary resource for educators teaching or reading Book I of the *Aeneid.* The complete text, an interlinear translation, complete metrical scansion, and an accompanying, more polished translation are just part of this goldmine. At the bottom of each page below the text, each Latin word is completely parsed. The commentary includes useful references to the revised grammars of Bennett, Gildersleeve, Allen and Greenough, and Harkness and delves into word derivations and word frequencies.

> . . . teachers, scholars, and non-experts can be confident that they are using the most thoroughly and reliably parsed text of Vergil in existence.
>
> – Ward W. Briggs, Jr.

iv + 348 pp. (2005, reprint of 1899, 1901 edition) 6" x 9" Paperback, ISBN 978-0-86516-630-1

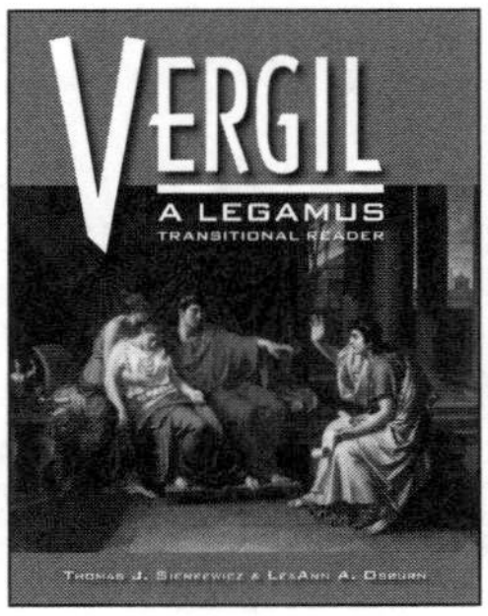

Vergil: A LEGAMUS Transitional Reader

Thomas J. Sienkewicz and LeaAnn A. Osburn

11 selections (about 200 lines) from Vergil's *Aeneid,* Books I, II, and IV, designed for students moving from elementary or intermediate Latin into reading authentic Vergilian Latin. Many reading aids, introductory materials, illustrations, and a grammatical appendix.

Features: • Pre- and post-materials help students understand underlying cultural/literary concepts and Vergil's style • Short explanations of grammar/syntax, with exercises • 1st version of Latin text has • gapped words in parentheses • difficult noun-adjective pairings highlighted • complete vocabulary/grammatical notes on facing page • 2nd version of Latin text in its unchanged form has literary notes on facing page • 3 concluding Latin passages with facing-page notes on grammar, vocabulary, and literary analysis, but without transitional aids • Pull-out end vocabulary for unglossed items

xxiv + 136 pp. (2004) 8 ½" x 11" Paperback, ISBN 978-0-86516-578-6

*AP is a registered trademark of the College Entrance Examination Board, which was not involved in the production of, and does not endorse, this product.

Bolchazy-Carducci Publishers, Inc.
www.BOLCHAZY.com

THE ART OF THE AENEID, 2nd edition

William S. Anderson

Anderson's text captures both the toughness and the tenderness of the greatest work of Latin literature. Includes examinations of each book of the *Aeneid,* extensive notes, suggestions for further reading, and a Vergil chronology.

> The classic book for English readers of *The Aeneid.*
>
> –*American Journal of Philology*

viii + 121 (1969, 2nd edition 2005) Paperback, ISBN 978-0-86516-598-4

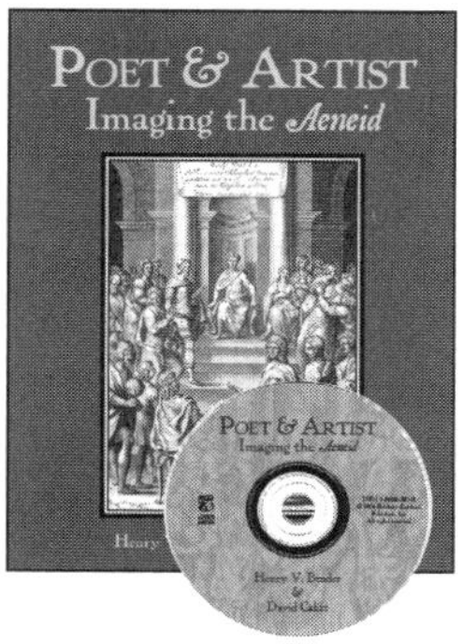

POET & ARTIST: Imaging the *Aeneid*

Henry V. Bender and David Califf

Book/CD combination that juxtaposes images with the AP* text of Vergil and thought-provoking questions. Encourages students to examine the text more closely and reflect more critically upon it.

Features: • Complete text of all lines on the Vergil AP* syllabus • All of Ogilby's plates on CD rom • Questions in English that require the students to compare and contrast Vergil's Latin text with the illustrations on the CD

xvi + 88 pp. (2004) 8 ½" x 11" Paperback + CD-ROM, ISBN 978-0-86516-585-4

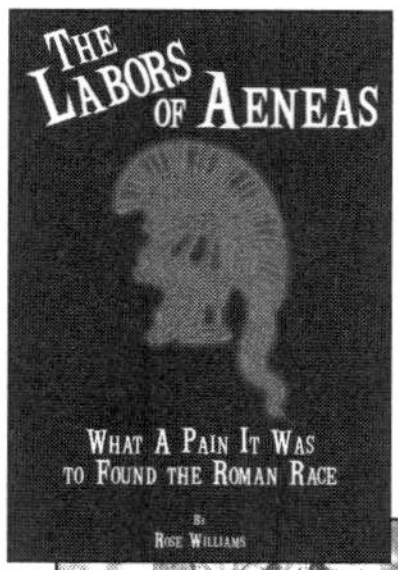

THE LABORS OF AENEAS: What A Pain It Was to Found the Roman Race

Rose Williams

The Labors of Aeneas is a delightful retelling of Vergil's *Aeneid* that has changed the tone, but not the tale. Ever-faithful to the story's facts, Rose Williams recounts Vergil's epic in a modern's voice—in witty, droll fashion.

Features: • The story of *The Aeneid,* Books I–XII, retold • Black and white illustrations • Notes • A glossary of gods prominent in *The Aeneid*

vi + 108 pp. (2003) 6" x 9" Paperback, ISBN 978-0-86516-556-4

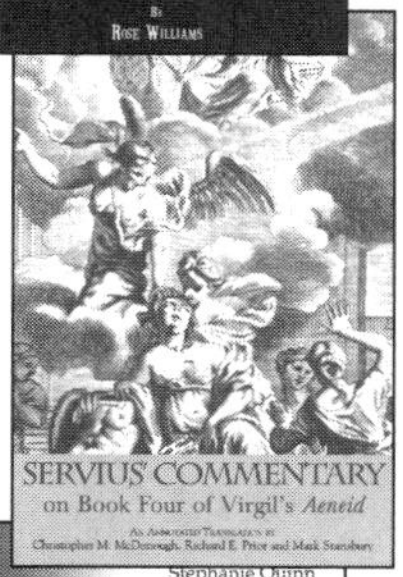

SERVIUS' COMMENTARY on Book Four of Virgil's *Aeneid*

An Annotated Translation

Christopher M. McDonough, Richard E. Prior, and Mark Stansbury

Servius' Commentary is important not only as a source of information on Virgil's poem but also for its countless gems about Roman life and literature. Its value has remained unquestioned.

Features: • Frontispiece: Facsimile page from the 1536 edition of Servius' commentary on Book 4 • Introduction on the life of Servius and the textual tradition • Latin text of Virgil's *Aeneid,* Book 4, with Servius' Commentary below • Facing-page English translation of both Virgil and Servius • Endnotes • Guide to further reading

xviii + 170 pp. (2004) 6" x 9" Paperback, ISBN 978-0-86516-514-4

WHY VERGIL? A Collection of Interpretations

Stephanie Quinn, ed.

43 selections by 38 authors including: • W. H. Auden • Herbert W. Bernario • D. C. Feeney • Robert Frost • Erich S. Gruen • W. R. Johnson • Bernard M. W. Knox • Brooks Otis • Michael C. J. Putnam • Meyer Reinhold • Charles Segal • Marilyn B. Skinner

> Stephanie Quinn's collection should benefit anyone interested in the study and understanding of Vergil, regardless of one's level of expertise in the Vergilian text.
>
> –Sophia Papaioannou, *Texas Classics in Action*

(2000) Paperback, ISBN 978-0-86516-418-5 • Hardbound, ISBN 978-0-86516-435-2

*AP is a registered trademark of the College Entrance Examination Board, which was not involved in the production of, and does not endorse, this product.

BOLCHAZY-CARDUCCI PUBLISHERS, INC.
WWW.BOLCHAZY.COM

Vergil for Beginners

A Dual Approach to Early Vergil Study

Rose Williams

This ancillary text for first-year high school Latin students or for students beginning their second semester of college Latin presents six short selections from Vergil's *Aeneid,* each accompanied by grammar exercises and vocabulary aids.

The design of the book works for either grammar-based or reading-based approaches, or some mixture of the two. The different sections in the book can be used in whatever order the teacher finds most effective. Grammar exercises present and review key elements of grammar for each reading selection, and Latin synonyms promote reading comprehension. The use of this reading supplement near the end of students' most basic Latin study will help the students develop the ability to handle Latin literature as they reach an advanced level.

Student Text: xii + 96 pp. (2006) 6" x 9" Paperback, ISBN 978-0-86516-628-8
Teacher's Guide: (forthcoming) ISBN 978-0-86516-629-5

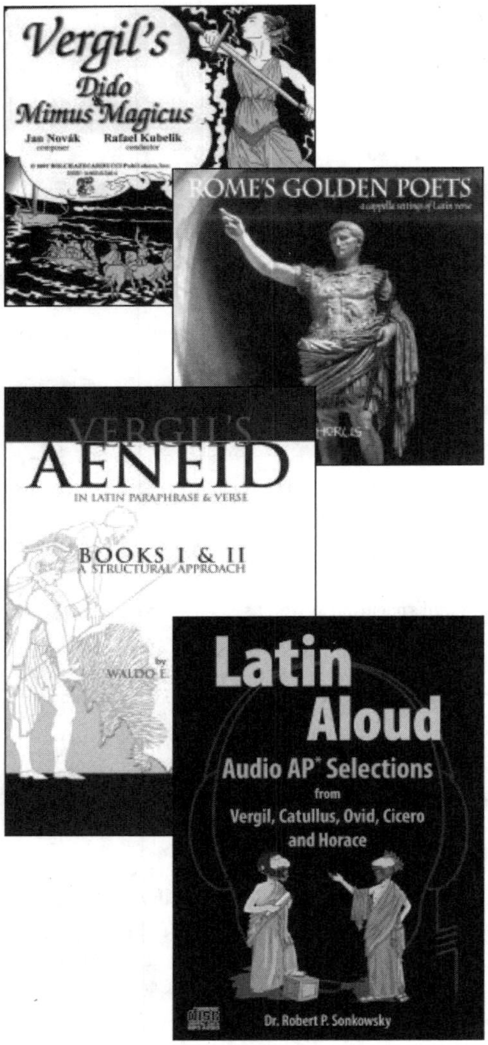

Vergil's Dido & Mimus Magicus

Composed by Jan Novák; Conducted by Rafael Kubelik; Performed by the Symphony Orchestra of the Bayerischer Rundfunk; Original record published by audite Schallplatten, Germany

Adaptations of two famous Vergil passages: Dido (*Aeneid* IV) and Mimus Magicus (*Eclogue* VIII), in lively recited and beautifully sung Latin.

Limited Edition CD (1997) 40-page libretto in Latin, English, and German, ISBN 978-0-86516-346-1

Rome's Golden Poets

St. Louis Chamber Chorus

Selections from Catullus, Vergil, and Horace are performed by the St. Louis Chamber Chorus under the direction of Philip Barnes.

Limited edition CD, ISBN 978-0-86516-474-1

Vergil's Aeneid: Books I & II

Waldo E. Sweet

This book features a paraphrase in easy Latin facing the original to help students understand the plain meaning of the text. Also, instead of a typical Latin-to-English vocabulary, there are selected notes from Servius and others in Latin, explaining the words and phrases of the original.

163 pp. (1960, Reprint 1983) Paperback, ISBN 978-0-86516-023-1

Latin Aloud

Audio AP* Selections from Vergil, Catullus, Ovid, Cicero, and Horace

read by Robert P. Sonkowsky

Vergil Features: • Vergil AP* Selections – Aeneid, Georgics, Eclogues
• Tracks broken into individual poems, odes, and digestible portions of longer works.
• Contains nearly all of the readings on the AP Latin syllabus. • Accompanies any of Bolchazy-Carducci's AP Latin readers and workbooks.

CD (2008) UPC: 00007

Bolchazy-Carducci Publishers, Inc.
www.BOLCHAZY.com